WALLFLOWERS IN THE KINGDOM

Other Books by Louis N. Jones

Equipping Your Church to Minister to Ex-Offenders
I Need a J-O-B!
Prodigal in the City
The Colors Will Change
Adverse Possession

WALLFLOWERS IN THE KINGDOM:
A Vindication of Introverts in the Body of Christ

Louis N. Jones

CONQUEST PUBLISHERS

Conquest Publishers
A division of Conquest Industries, LLC
P.O. Box 611
Bladensburg, MD 20710-0611
www.conquestpublishers.com

ISBN 13: 978-0-9883809-2-9

Library of Congress Control Number: 2012922876

Printed in the United States of America

Although this book chronicles true events and actual persons, the names of the people have been changed to preserve their privacy.

It is obvious that God loves variety—just look around! He cre-
ated each of us with a unique combination of personality traits.
God made introverts and extroverts. He made people who love
routine and those who love variety. He made some people
"thinkers" and others "feelers." Some people work best when
given an individual assignment while others work better with a
team. The Bible says, "God works through different people in
different ways, but it is the same God who achieves his purpose
through them all" (I Corinthians 12:6, New Testament in Modern English *by J. B. Phillips, New York: Macmillan, 1958.).*

From *The Purpose Driven Life*, Rick Warren, 2002

"My attitude to these matters is that, as long as a patient is re-
ally a member of a church, he ought to be serious. He ought to
be really and sincerely a member of that church, and he should
not go to a doctor to get his conflicts settled when he believes
that he should do it with God. For instance, when a member of
the Oxford Group comes to me in order to get treatment, I say,
'You are in the Oxford Group; so long as you are there, you
settle your affair with the Oxford Group.' I can't do it better
than Jesus."[1]

---

1   Carl Jung, *The Symbolic Life*, p. 272.

CONTENTS

Forced social encounters

Educate your church leaders about temperament.
Join or start a small group.
Participate in creative arts ministries.
Social networking or online participation.
Mentoring and Discipleship.
Preaching and teaching.
Become accountable.
Try not to fit in.
Prayer and meditation.
Seek to understand extroverts.

Preface

One of the constant mantras in any writer's life is to "write what you know." This book is a thorough biblical examination of introversion—something I have experienced for most of my life that I have fruitlessly tried to morph into something more socially acceptable. This book is an expression of my calling and an effort to make peace with how God created me. It is my hope and prayer that if you have obtained this book and you are an introvert, that you will read it prayerfully and realize that God has created you to be special, and that introverts no longer have to take a backseat to extroverts.

I have borrowed the term *introvert* from the psychological field. However, this book does not focus primarily on a psychological and scientific discussion of introversion. Many books on the market provide such information. The information in this book flows from my experiences as an introvert, and from careful study of the word of God. *Introversion* is the most appropriate term to describe a personality type that was created by God and was in existence long before Carl Jung or anyone else decided to study it. Therefore, my intent here is not to provide a psychological treatise embellished with theology. It is to provide a theological examination of introversion supported by psychology.

I also realize that in writing this, my experiences as an introvert may not be typical of other introverts, and may vary depending upon the degrees of introversion that are in each person. The information in this book should be used as a guide for self-reflection and should be accompanied by prayer and counseling. It should not be used as a means to make any psychological or spiritual diagnoses. Also, if you are involved in an extroverted church, career, or family, the information in this book should not be interpreted as an endorsement to separate from these endeavors. Again, much prayer and counseling with a qualified pastoral counselor is required before making any determinations. It is essential that, even if you find information in this book that resonates with your situation, you follow the leading of the Holy Spirit regarding his call and direction for your life.

I say here (and I will mention it a few other times in this book) that this vindication of introverts is not intended to make villains of extroverts. It is my position that *both* introverts and extroverts have value in the kingdom of God, and that there is nothing wrong with either one. The audience for this book is not just introverts in the process of self-discovery. This book is also for extroverts who want to understand introverts better. It is for those who minister to introverts, and for those who are in relationships with introverts. My hope and prayer is that a better understanding of this personality type will lead to more fruitful relationships in the body of Christ, and will further enhance the kingdom's ability to minister to the saints and win souls to the kingdom.

Finally, I am aware that other books about introversion are out there, some with more authoritative voices than mine. I know of at least one other book that deals with introversion in the body of Christ. I have not read these books, so if there is any similarity to them, it is only because of my understanding of the subject matter. I do not take away from any of these works. This book is my voice and an integral part of my journey to understand how God has made me. I want to live the rest of my life with that understanding.

Defining Introversion

The word *introvert* is not a biblical term. However, its lack of presence in the Bible does not invalidate its use any more than the lack of the word "lettuce" means we cannot eat it. Its source is controversial for some Christians, especially those who believe that psychology is antithetical to biblical Christianity. I do not share that view entirely. Psychology is the study of the *psyche*, or the soul, and some benefit has been derived from its science. However, I do not believe that psychology presents a full view of the human personality, and that is where the Bible comes in. The Bible is more than just a book of fancy writing. It is God's written instructions to humankind, inspired by the Holy Spirit. No study of the soul and the mind can be complete without tapping into the

Spirit of God.

The Swiss psychologist Carl Jung first popularized the term *introversion*. Jung did not discover introversion. He merely placed a label on a type of behavior that he had observed through years of study.

In the 1980s, I worked and fellowshipped with members of the Church of the Nazarene. I heard Jung's name mentioned frequently among them in casual conversations, because his teachings were quite influential in those circles. Today, Jung's psychology-based teachings and theories, particularly the Myers-Briggs Type Indicator®, remain influential, even among some Christians.

However, many Christians are quick to label Jung a pagan, an idolater, and an occultist. And much is written about Jung to support those opinions. Therefore, many people in the Christian community, especially those within charismatic circles, reject Jung's theories and, in some cases, the whole notion of psychology. They believe that God and the Holy Spirit make any such theories irrelevant. This is why the use of the word *introversion* within Christian circles remains controversial. In some cases, the term is rejected outright.

I want to make it clear that I am neither a student nor a faithful adherent of Jung's theories. I have completed very little study of him, other than to learn about his coining of the word introversion. He is mentioned here only as a historical reference to introversion, and as a person who studied and placed a name on a human quality that I believe is God-given. But the question is, if something is discovered by a person with questionable moral character, does that nullify or disqualify the discovery?

Not necessarily. For if the answer to that question is yes, moral-minded Christians would have to reject or repudiate most discoveries known to man, including a sizable amount of the foods we eat.

In his studies, Jung found something inherent in the souls of many men and women that was not secret, but was in place far before Jung and that transcends any natural understanding. My premise in this book is that God created introverts that way, and it is only through the word of God that "quiet people" can truly be understood.

Since the word introversion is not in the Bible, we lack a definition from that source. So, please humor the following definition of introversion from Wikipedia[2]:

Introversion is "the state of or tendency toward being wholly or predominantly concerned with and interested in one's own mental life." Introverts are people whose energy tends to expand through reflection and dwindle during interaction. Introverts tend to be more reserved and less outspoken in large groups. They often take pleasure in solitary activities such as reading, writing, music, drawing, tinkering, playing video games, watching movies and plays, and using

2   http://en.wikipedia.org/wiki/Extraversion_and_introversion

computers, along with some more reserved outdoor activities, such as fishing. In fact, social networking sites have been a thriving home for introverts in the twenty-first century, where introverts are free from the formalities of social conduct and may become more comfortable about personal feelings they would not otherwise disclose. The archetypal artist, writer, sculptor, engineer, composer and inventor are all highly introverted. An introvert is likely to enjoy time spent alone and find less reward in time spent with large groups of people, though he or she may enjoy interactions with close friends. Trust is usually an issue of significance: a virtue of utmost importance to an introvert choosing a worthy companion. They prefer to concentrate on a single activity at a time and like to observe situations before they participate, especially observed in developing children and adolescents. Introverts are easily overwhelmed by too much stimulation from social gatherings and engagement. They are more analytical before speaking.

Introversion is often determined through several psychological instruments. The most popular and widely accepted of these instruments is the Myers-Briggs Type Indicator®, which classifies people into sixteen different personality types. I took an adapted version of this test a few years ago as part of a course on learning how to manage people with varying personality types. The test revealed that I was an INFJ (Introverted, Intuitive, Feeling, Judging). The definition of INFJ follows:

INFJs are future oriented, and direct their insight and inspiration toward the understanding of themselves and thereby human nature. Their works mirror their integrity, and it needs to reflect their inner ideals. Solitude and an opportunity to concentrate thoroughly on what counts most are important to them. INFJs prefer to quietly exert their influence. They have deeply felt compassion, and they desire harmony with others. INFJs understand the complexities existing within people and among them. They do not call a great deal of attention to themselves, preferring that their contributions speak for them. They are at their best concentrating on their ideas, ideals, and inspirations.[3]

While there is debate among Christians as to the morality and validity of these tests (the opinions range from recommending them as essential to dismissing them as tools of the occult), I cannot deny that the result of the test was quite an accurate description of my personality.[4] The results of the test

3   Jen M. Kummerow, Nancy J. Barger, and Linda K. Kirby. *Work Types* (Warner Books, Inc., 1997), 20.

4   Because the Myers-Briggs Type Indicator® and other similar tests present a snapshot "point-in-time" picture of one's personality, and because the activity of the Holy Spirit can and often does change personality, or brings out a more dormant aspect of personality depending on the situation, I cannot recommend the use of these tests to inform decisions in a kingdom ministry capacity. They are mentioned here only to define a particular personality type, but should not be understood as an endorsement of their methodologies.

also indicated that two of my suitable career types were literature or writing, and social service, particularly religious education. I happen to be a minister and a writer. Coincidence? Likely not.

Defining the Kingdom

Now that we have a working understanding of introversion and the origin of the word, let's turn to another word that can be just as controversial. In this book, I will make several references to the kingdom of God. I use this term primarily to differentiate between ordinary Christians and those who are kingdom Christians. There are over 2.1 billion Christians in the world. However, I believe the number of kingdom Christians, according to biblical definition, is decidedly smaller. I share this opinion based on my own observations and not on any official study (although it is unlikely that there has been an official study on the number of kingdom Christians).

Below are two key scriptures that define the kingdom of God:

> *Being asked by the Pharisees when the kingdom of God would come, he answered them, "The kingdom of God does not come with your careful observation, nor will they say, 'Look, here it is!' or 'There it is,' for behold, the kingdom of God is within you" (Luke 17:20-21).*

"Not everyone who says to me, 'Lord, Lord,' will enter the kingdom of heaven, but the one who does the will of my Father who is in heaven" (Matthew 7:21).

The terms "kingdom of heaven" and "kingdom of God" are used interchangeably and are identical in meaning. Together, these two scriptures give us a very good working definition of the kingdom of God.

As St. Luke states, the kingdom of God cannot be observed. It has no geographical boundaries. It has no definition or classification. It is, however, in our midst, or inside of us. According to Matthew chapter 7, people enter the kingdom of God by doing the will of God. The dictionary meaning of the word "kingdom" is the reign of a king. We can conclude from this that the kingdom of God is total and complete submission and obedience to God. We allow the Holy Spirit to operate inside us to bring us under subjection to the rule and reign of God. We acknowledge his lordship and authority over our lives.

Isn't this what being a Christian means? Yes, but

the meaning escapes some people who call themselves Christian. These people see Christ only as a
figurehead, someone to obey only when it is conve-
nient to do so. They continue to live with unrepen-
tant sin in their lives. They function and make decisions according to their own selfish desires. They
live in the flesh, and have no patience for the things
of the Spirit.

On the contrary, the kingdom of God is Christ's
unshakable and unchangeable rule and reign over
us. It is possible to be a Christian in name only, but
not submitted to the lordship of Christ. As Matthew
writes, *"Not everyone who says to me, 'Lord, Lord,' will
enter the kingdom of heaven."* For those who desire to
enter the kingdom of God, the word "Lord" cannot
be used frivolously or as empty jargon. It must become real to us. When we say, "Lord" in reference to
Christ, our hearts must be in agreement with what
we are saying. When we say "Lord" and mean it,
we are submitting our lives to the rule and reign of
Christ. We are no longer mediocre Christians. We
are loyal subjects in his kingdom.

The scripture in Luke 17 also implies something
that I believe is important in understanding the kingdom. The scripture says that the kingdom of God is
"in the midst of you." If something is in my midst, it
means that it is here — and that it is accessible to me at
present. The kingdom of God is *here and now*. It is not
a future event. It is not something that will happen
at some predetermined date. The kingdom is pres-

ent and real. And while I believe that there will be a future reign of Christ (Isaiah 11:6-9), there is also a present reign — one to which believers are completely and totally submitted.

I define the term because this book will likely have no value to those who have not submitted their lives to the rule and reign of Christ and are not interested in doing so. This book is for a church that has committed itself to do whatever the Lord wills, through the ministry of the Holy Spirit.

My Experiences as an Introvert

I am an introvert. And I am proud of it.

I became comfortable with my introversion only a few months before writing this book. I had always known that I was not as socially outgoing as others, and a bit of a loner at times. As a child, I spent most of my indoor time in my room engaged in some creative project or another. I did not go out of my way to attend parties. I had a few friends, but certainly not as many as other kids in the neighborhood. I had a tendency to keep my thoughts to myself. If I didn't like someone, he or she never would have heard it from me.

And yes, I suffered as a result. Girls tended to be more attracted to the outgoing, gregarious types and would barely pay me any attention. Because of my studiousness, I was called a bookworm, which was intended as a term of derision. Because I was quiet and didn't talk much, there was a sense of mystery about me. I learned later that people generally do not trust mysterious people. Because mysterious people share so little of themselves, others are often left with many questions. *What they are thinking? What is their mentality? What are they up to? Are they crazy? What are they hiding?* Many people find it difficult to put their full trust in someone they know nothing about. "Watch out for the quiet ones" or "pay attention to the quiet ones" are common sayings sometimes applied negatively to shy people and introverts[5]. The implication is, "watch them. They cannot be trusted."

Because I did not "beat my chest" and express wanton male physicality like so many of the other boys, I was often the target of bullying. Bullies like to pick on people that they perceive as weak. If I had conducted myself as a tough guy who would slap you silly if you approached me the wrong way, I would have waylaid many a bully without having to lift a finger.

Now that I am older, many of the traits that were present in me as a kid are still there, although much of the shyness (which is not necessarily the same as introversion) has disappeared. For additional discussion, refer to the section "Am I Shy, an Introvert,

---

5   There is also a positive spin to these sayings, which can be interpreted as, "Watch out for the quiet ones. They will be your friends when everyone else is gone."

or Both?"

Of course, it wasn't all bad. In fact, one major positive aspect of my introversion has affected my life to this day. Because of my quiet nature and my desire not to be "the life of the party," I steered clear of the "in" crowd and the people who were engaged in boisterous and often destructive activity. In my inner-city neighborhood of Washington, D.C., to be "in" was to involve oneself with all kinds of questionable behavior and to align oneself with the shady morals and values of that crowd.

I remember a few attempts at trying to break out of my introversion and be more popular. One of the most memorable ones occurred when I was attending Cardozo High School in Northwest Washington, D.C. The school was only a four-minute walk from the apartment where my mother and I lived. I met "Marlene" through one of my male friends, and we also became friends. Marlene was not pretty enough for me to be attracted to her, and we didn't hang out much (I learned later in life that it was not appropriate to judge by appearances). However, she had another female friend, "Shelly," whom I thought was gorgeous. The two were practically joined at the hip, so I wanted to spend more time with Marlene just to have a chance at hooking up with Shelly.

One day during lunch, Marlene, accompanied by Shelly, mentioned that she wanted a Bacardi rum and Coke, a very popular alcoholic drink among teenagers at the time. I was seventeen and had accepted the

Lord Jesus Christ as my savior about two years earlier, but never followed through on my commitment to him. I knew about my mother's liquor cabinet at home, and that it contained Bacardi rum. All we had to do was go to the corner convenience store and buy Cokes, and we were all set. And since Shelly was with Marlene, I would have done almost anything to spend some more time with her.

I invited the girls over to my apartment. There, we poured Bacardi rum and Coke for each of us and drank them at the kitchen table (we used small glasses, as we were smart enough to avoid getting drunk in the middle of the school day). That was it. We went back to school, and no one was the wiser. We repeated these lunchtime trysts several times, until the Bacardi was almost exhausted. I experienced a slight uptick in popularity and street cred because I was hanging out with these two cool girls at my home, and the girls likely told all their friends that we were drinking liquor. So, probably half the kids at school knew about it. How my mother never knew about this is a mystery (although, if she is like most mothers, she either figured it out, or she blamed someone else in the family who was more likely to do such a thing). But if she knew I did it, for some reason she just never let on that she knew.

The memory of this event causes me to give thanks to God, because it could have been a lot worse. Because of my momentary desire to fit in, I might have become addicted, and might have completely destroyed my life because of incessant use and abuse of alcohol. Alcohol is one of the leading causes of death among teenagers, and I might easily have been one of the statistics.[6] Praise God that it did not turn out that way.

There were other danger areas, too. My desire to hook up with Shelly, had it worked out the way I wanted it to, might have resulted in my getting a sexually transmitted disease. Or I might have ended up having to support and raise a child at seventeen. I completely violated the trust that my mother placed in me, and I completely abandoned almost every principle that I learned in the few Bible studies I had participated in when I was actively attending church a couple of years before.

So, when I think of this and other attempts to fit in, I thank God that most of them failed. My desire to fit in was short-lived. I just wanted to get back to the person I was at the time—the studious introvert.

So, I was fully aware of my introversion from childhood through adulthood (although I had no idea that it was called introversion). And my personality type has its ups and downs. For instance, I remember being considered for a promotion to a job that I was fully qualified for. But the director of human resources, after an interview with me, told me

6   *Ninth Special Report to the U.S. Congress on Alcohol and Health from the Secretary of Health and Human Services.* Rockville, MD: USDHHS, Public Health Service, Alcohol, Drug Abuse and Mental Health Administration, National Institute on Alcohol Abuse and Alcoholism, Jun 1997.

directly that I would not be considered further for the position because I was not "aggressive" enough. Apparently, the job required a more take-charge, less laid-back sort of person. I couldn't imagine how a job in the accounting department, sitting in front of a computer all day, required an aggressive person, but perhaps there were some aspects of that job that I did not understand.

I have lived most of my life being an introvert. But I became comfortable with being an introvert after a few days of self-reflection — just a few months before this book was written. The event triggering the self-reflection happened during my tenure as a nonprofit organization manager. I had walked into a room divided in two by a wall of cubicles. Employees were in the cubicles talking, but because the cubicles had no line of sight to the area I had entered, the people in the cubicles had no idea that I was there.

In this room were several bookshelves that we use to store books we place online for sale. I went to the bookshelf to retrieve a book for a customer, just like I had done countless times over the year I had worked for this organization. But on my way out, after hearing one employee mention my name, it became apparent that the people in the cubicles were talking about *me*.

This may sound strange, but I did what many people probably would *not* have done. Instead of staying just long enough to listen without being discovered, I continued to walk out of the room and did not listen to the conversation any further.

As I thought about that moment, I realized that I have a sensitive nature and that I am particularly sensitive to hearing criticism about myself. Some people, when someone calls them names or says negative or critical things about them, can dismiss those things quickly, particularly if they come from strangers. In my case, even if a stranger says negative things about me, I will think about it for *days*. My sensitive and introspective nature will cause me to process these negative comments and determine if there is anything in me that would make these comments legitimate. Is there a malady in me? Is there something that needs changing? Introverted people are more likely to analyze themselves in this way.

Because of my sensitive nature, these types of comments are hurtful — at least initially. That's why I walked out of the room. I had no desire to be hurt by hearing negative comments about me.

But who's to say that the comments about me were negative? They may have been as complimentary as any praise I have ever received. But I didn't stick around long enough to find out; I didn't want to take any chances.

After this incident, I came to grips with myself, with the help of some self-reflection and a lot of praying. I am an introvert. I am quiet, reserved, and sensitive. I have been that way since childhood, and the Lord made me that way. Although my lifestyle involves attending meeting after meeting and social event after social event, I am perfectly comfortable staying on the periphery of these encounters. In meetings with several people at once, I will listen intently, but will not speak unless I have something very insightful and relevant to say. If I hear that a meeting is highly interactive, that is usually a reason for me to find some excuse not to attend.

Some people go to meetings and talk because they are expected to talk, because they want to prove themselves knowledgeable, influential, and insightful, or because they want to be the center of attention. They may have several other motivations. As an introvert, I have no such motivations. I am perfectly comfortable being the only one in the room not saying anything, avoiding the temptation to talk just to be talking. If I have something to say, I will say it. If I have a question to ask, I will ask it. But do not expect any grandstanding or filibusters from me. It is not in an introvert's nature.

I understand why I can go to a church meeting for three hours and be totally drained by the time it is over. Yet, once I get home, suddenly I am the Energizer Bunny® for two more hours. I understand why I loathe the fast-paced life, jetting around from place to place, having several meetings in one day. I understand why I have to frequently tell people, "I'll think about it," when I am asked to respond to something, and get the condescending looks — as if it is a major crime to not be able to think on one's feet and come up with quick answers. I now understand why my observation and listening skills are so well developed.

I am an introvert. And I am proud of it.

Extroverts Need Love, too!!

In writing this book, I want to make it clear that I am not seeking to demonize extroverts. Just as introverts have their positive and negative qualities, so do extroverts. Just because a quality of an introvert is positive, does not mean that the opposite quality in an extrovert is negative. Both extroverts and introverts have an equal amount of positive qualities and negative qualities. God has used introverts and extroverts to achieve his purposes. This is one of the beauties of the kingdom of God. People of various personalities, cultures, upbringings, and circumstances all come together, worship together, and love one another as family. We are related to one another through the bloodline of Jesus Christ.

The Christian Wallflower

wallflower - perennial of southern Europe having clusters of fragrant flowers of all colors especially yellow and orange; often naturalized on old walls or cliffs; sometimes placed in genus *Erysimum*

I have never taken Gardening 101, but even with my limited knowledge of flowers, shrubs, and herbs, I am certain that an old wall or cliff would not be my ideal location for starting a garden. Yet, the indomitable wallflower finds a way to grow and prosper in circumstances where most garden plants would not stand a chance. It grows in these dry areas, undaunted, isolated from much of the garden; yet it is just as stately, fragrant, and beautiful as any other plant in the garden.

Given the plant's natural habitat, the use of its name is perfect to describe individuals who are too withdrawn to mingle with the crowd at social gatherings. Isolated from the life of the party, they linger against the wall, staying away from the action. They are stereotyped as antisocial, aloof, or weird. They watch the goings-on, but rarely blend in. Few people give them attention. Yet, just like the perennial of Europe, they are often as beautiful and fragrant as any other person in the room.

In this context, the term *wallflower*, as applied to shy and introverted people, is not derisive, but rather a badge of honor that recognizes their tendency to isolate themselves; however, they have just as much to offer as anyone else. Many people who have established relationships with shy and introverted people say that they are some of the most wonderful people they have ever met.

So, why are shy and introverted people having such a difficult time in the kingdom of God?

In writing this book, I relate, in no small degree, to my own experiences as an introverted person. Even as a minister and an assistant pastor, I feel as though I do not fit in sometimes. I go to meetings and gatherings where people often talk for hours about the Word of God, yet I do not have much to say. It is not that I do not know the Word or study the Word, nor am I afraid to speak up. But I am, simply, a man of few words. I often struggle to come up with enough words to fill an entire conversation.

I enjoy church. I enjoy fellowshipping with the saints of God, and I find that I would rather be among the saints than at a nightclub, a bar, or some other secular gathering place where I would *really* not fit in. But as much as I enjoy it, I can only enjoy it for so long. Not that there is anything wrong with the people I fellowship with. I think that they are some of the most wonderful people in the world. They have become like a second family to me, and my church is small enough so that I know everyone by name. But after a while, I start to yearn for some alone time — for time spent in solitude or in the company of one or more friends.

I don't like crowds; I never have. I will drive miles away to shop at a less-crowded store than shop at one that is packed with people and is only a few city blocks away. Most of my shopping trips are made at night, when the crowds have died down.

I have struggled with these tendencies for a long time. Sometimes I feel as if I am strange, or not a true follower of Christ. This is not self-deprecation; this is the environment that I find myself in.

Countries other than the United States of America place a higher value on introversion (China is one such country[7]), but the United States of America is largely an extroverted country. Many of its churches

7   "The Real Reason Chinese Mothers Are Superior," published by Susan Cain in her book, "QUIET: The Power of Introverts in a World That Can't Stop Talking," which also appeared in *Psychology Today* on April 28, 2011

are also extroverted, although a few exceptions exist. I belong to a church that is largely evangelical. In an evangelical church, if members are not sharing the Lord Jesus Christ with others, usually through direct speaking or preaching, then they are not functioning in God's will for their lives. In an evangelical church, if people are not sharing the gospel, then something is wrong with them. They are not functioning in the will of God.

In sermon after sermon, teaching after teaching, sharing Jesus with others is often emphasized, particularly with those outside the church. The scripture supports this theory when it says in Matthew 28:19-20: *"Therefore go and make disciples of all nations, baptizing them in the name of the Father and of the Son and of the Holy Spirit, and teaching them to obey everything I have commanded you. And surely I am with you always, to the very end of the age."*

For extroverts, this is easy. They go out, meet people, strike up conversations, and tell others about Jesus. For introverts like me, this can be a struggle. We are not the types to go out and begin conversations with people we don't know. We are usually not the types to initiate relationships. For introverts, it is difficult to find ways to live out this scripture in the context of an evangelical, extroverted church environment. And this may leave introverts with a sense of inadequacy, lack of belonging, and a feeling of being ostracized — despite the good intentions of those within the church.

The natural response to this is to say that introverted people need to change in order to live out the scripture. In other words, introverted people need to function and behave like extroverts. And that is the issue. In an extroverted environment, the typical advice to introverts is to tell them that they need to change, that introversion is against scripture, and that they need to become bolder in Christ.

But what if God doesn't want them to change? What if introversion is an inherent aspect of their personalities, and is an element of who God made them to be? What if God created introverts for a special purpose, just as he created extroverts for a special purpose?

To answer that question, let's take a closer look at God's created genius, the human being, and how personality and introversion and extroversion fit into his creation.

The Seat of Personality

Personality
1. *The quality or condition of being a person.*
2. *The totality of qualities and traits, as of character or behavior, that is peculiar to a specific person.*

Psalm 139:13-14
For you created my inmost being; you knit me

together in my mother's womb. I praise you because I am fearfully and wonderfully (uniquely) made; your works are wonderful, I know that full well.

In this psalm, David is acknowledging God's handiwork in his life and the fact that he was created reverently and uniquely; uniquely not only in the sense of being a human distinct from the animals, but unique and distinct from other human beings. We need only look at our fingerprints, which are different from any other human, to know that God has created each of us uniquely. No two humans on the face of the earth are the same. He fashioned us from the foundation of the world to serve his purpose, and he has placed in us a distinct set of characteristics that enable us to live out the calling that he has placed on our lives.

Ephesians 2:10 states: *"For we are God's workmanship, created in Christ Jesus for good works, which God prepared in advance for us to do."* Each of us is a work of art, created uniquely by the Master for his will and purpose. No sculptor or painter creates a work of art and then fashions the same thing over and over. Each time he or she creates, the artist creates something different and distinct. No composer writes a song and then composes the same song again. Similarly, starting with Adam and Eve and continuing to this day, each human created by God is different from the other. Even in the case of identical twins who are simi-

lar biologically, each one develops different character patterns and personality traits throughout life. It
is fitting to borrow this idiom: "when God made us,
he broke the mold."

As we further examine God's handiwork, it is
pertinent to note that God said that we were "created in our image" (Genesis 1:26). The fact that God
uses the adjective "our" indicates that he is speaking
as part of a group. This triune nature of God is clari-
fied in Matthew 28:19, which states, *"Therefore go and
make disciples of all nations, baptizing them in the name
of the Father and of the Son and of the Holy Spirit."* This
illustrates that God has three distinct persons, or in-
dividualities, but is essentially in one body. Since we
are created in his image, that means that we also are
triune beings, comprised of body, soul, and spirit (1
Thessalonians 5:23).

The word "hypostasis" or "person," as used to describe each of the three elements of the triune God, is
interesting, as the word forms the basis for the word
personality. Neither the word *trinity* nor the word *person* is used in the Bible, but a Latin theologian used
them later to adequately describe the nature of God.[8]
The word *person* was likely derived from the Latin word *persona*, meaning *mask*. It was common in
Greek theater for actors to put on masks to portray
personalities other than their own. Who doesn't remember the smiling mask and the frowning mask,

8   History of the Doctrine of the Trinity, Religionfacts.com,
accessed July 19, 2012.

side by side, which have represented theater for many centuries? *Personality* simply means the composite of characteristics that comprise an individual. Each of God's persons has a set of individual characteristics that make it distinct from the others. Each of God's hypostases has a distinct personality.

While human creation does not have three separate personalities, all the elements of our triune nature play a part in defining our personalities and making each human being distinct from any other human on the face of the earth. And, just as God's three persons form one entity and relate to one another in unity, the three elements of our triune nature — body, soul, and spirit — are united to formulate our personalities and determine our individual temperaments.

The Body, Soul, and Spirit—And how they relate to our Personalities

The Body

The body[9] is the mortal, physical aspect of us. It is the part of us that needs feeding, bathing, and exercise. It is the part of us that engages most with the environment around us. It allows us to work, to build, to hug, to worship. It is the outworking of all that God desires to do with us in this life. In the Old Tes-

9   From the Greek *soma*, meaning "the body, as a sound whole." (*The Hebrew-Greek Study Bible*, New American Standard, 1984).

tament, it is referred to as the "flesh."

The words *flesh* and *body* often have such negative connotations that it is troublesome at times to accept that the body is a crucial and important aspect of our person. But 1 Corinthians 6:19 says that the body is *"a temple of the Holy Spirit, who is in you."* In Romans 12:1, the body is denoted as the place of worship. Clearly the body is important, but it is nonetheless weak and subject to temptation (Matthew 26:41).

The body is intrinsically related to the soul and the spirit. Consequently, what affects the body will also affect the soul and the spirit. For instance, some people who are afflicted with a debilitating disease go through emotional turmoil. They may experience depression, and may become suicidal, while others, faced with the same disease, may deepen their faith and become more diligent at connecting with God through worship, praise, and prayer.

The body involved in sexual immorality will also affect the soul and the spirit. Consider 1 Corinthians 6:15-17:

> *Do you not know that your bodies are members of Christ himself? Shall I then take the members of Christ and unite them with a prostitute? Never! Do you not know that he who unites himself with a prostitute is one with her in body? For it is said, "The two will become one flesh." But he who unites himself with the Lord is one with him in spirit.*

Reading this scripture, it is easy to form a picture of a sexual sinner and a prostitute, joined together like Siamese twins, one in the flesh. But that is not what the scripture is saying. A better analogy would be a marriage. Married people typically share everything: a home, their food, their money, and their bodies. For one partner to link his or her body with the other partner, it creates a connection to the soul and spirit of the other partner. So, to join bodies with someone who may be spiritually bankrupt and morally deficient produces a negative effect on the entirety of the personality—such that God warns us to "*[f]lee from sexual immorality*" (1 Corinthians 6:18).

The effects are numerous and devastating. Guilt, shame, distrust, disease, addiction, and perversion are all results of a life lived in sexual immorality. Many people think that it is just sex, a physical joining of two physical bodies. It's a great feeling for a few minutes. But the impact is far greater.

The Soul

> *And the* LORD *God formed man of the dust of the ground, and breathed into his nostrils the breath of life; and man became a living soul (Genesis 2:7, KJV).*

The soul is the essence, the vitality, and the life

and breath of a person—breathed by God into the physical body of a man or woman. It is the seat of affections, emotions, the desire, and the will. In the New Testament, it is expressed by the Greek term *psūchê* *(psyche)*, which is the root of the word *psychology*.

In this aspect of mankind resides much of what makes a person an introvert. The will of a person, residing in the soul, is what often drives the actions of the person. For this reason, Satan is especially interested in attacking the soul—particularly the will. If he can influence the soul, the entire body will follow his bidding.

The things that we do in life, the subjects we are interested in, the hobbies that we pursue, the careers that we choose, the things that make us laugh, and the things that make us cry are all directed and energized by the soul. Our worship, our joy, and our temperaments come from the soul (Luke 1:46-47). These things are breathed into us at birth, are developed throughout life, and can be influenced by our environments.

The Changeable Soul

> *And the* LORD *God formed man of the dust of the ground, and breathed into his nostrils the breath of life; and man became a living soul (Genesis 2:7, KJV).*

> *But the natural man does not receive the things of the Spirit of God, for they are foolishness to him; nor can he know them because they are spiritually discerned (1 Corinthians 2:14, NKJV).*

Countless people have educated themselves into believing what I'm about to say is nonsense. But I believe that just as God breathed life into the first man in Genesis, so God breathes life into us at conception and continues to do so throughout our lives. The breath of God in us prepares our souls and enables us to function successfully in God's will. God breathed every emotion, desire, will, and aspect of our individuality into us, such that each of us has our own unique temperament and personality. Some elements of our souls are developed as we go through life, and some are even dormant until a certain age or time. Because our individual environments can affect our souls, it is important that the kingdom Christian who desires to serve God spends time regularly in the presence of the Holy Spirit. I'll touch on that in a moment.

Let's compare our bodies to our souls for a moment. We cannot change whether we are male or female, African American, Caucasian, Hispanic, Latino, or Asian. We cannot change them, nor will God change them. These aspects of our physicality are with us for life.[10]

---

10   In making this statement, I am not ignorant of the surgical procedures available today which purport to change one's sex or

Yet, there are other aspects of our bodies that we *can* change. A person who eats well and works out frequently may have a muscular body. A person who eats high-calorie foods and is sedentary may be overweight. A person who abuses drugs and alcohol is damaging his or her body and adversely affecting its functions. He or she is causing the body to develop an addiction to the substances ingested. So, our bodies can change depending on how we treat them, and depending on our individual environments.

Our souls are the same way. God places aspects of our souls within us, and we cannot change them. These include the capability to learn; the need for love, family, and companionship; the ability to express the varying emotions of happiness, sadness, anger, fear, and grief; and our temperaments (God can change them, but we cannot). But other aspects, such as our will, our desires, and our talents, can be changed. Whether we like rock music or classical, spicy foods or only veggies, football or hockey, these tastes can be changed depending on our surroundings, our educational and social development, our age, our friends, etc.

Since introversion and extroversion are aspects of our temperaments that cannot be changed, we are stuck with however the Lord has created us. Introverts certainly have the capability to engage their will and behave as extroverts, and some have gone to

---

reassign one's sex. These procedures are artificial and do not change the essential nature of women or men.

great lengths to do so. But our temperaments are essential parts of our souls; trying to behave in a manner contradictory to our personalities is like wearing a pair of shoes that are too tight. You may appear as if you are getting away with it, but only you know how uncomfortable you really are.

The Spirit

> *For who among men knows the thoughts of a man except the man's spirit within him? In the same way no one knows the thoughts of God except the Spirit of God* (1 Corinthians 2:11).

The spirit (small *s*) should be distinguished from the Spirit of God (capital *S*), or the Holy Spirit. Just as every person has a body and a soul, every person has a spirit. The spirit is the empowering aspect of a person, and informs and energizes the body and the soul. In addition to the soul, it is closely identified with the thoughts, understanding, will, and emotions of a person and drives those changeable and unchangeable aspects of our personalities, which are present in the soul.

A while ago, I was having a conversation with a gentleman who told me that he never gets angry. In the literal sense, this is not true. Every human being, no matter his or her religion, has the emotion of anger present within the soul, and the capability to express it. However, what the gentleman was trying to say was that he never displays *out-of-control* anger. What angers a person, and how that anger is manifested, is directly under the control of the person's spirit.

Another example concerns a person's thinking. Obviously, every person has the capability of thought. The spirit of the person directly inspires whether those thoughts are good or evil. Philippians 4:8 states, *"Finally, brothers and sisters, whatever is true, whatever is noble, whatever is right, whatever is pure, whatever is lovely, whatever is admirable – if anything is excellent or praiseworthy – think about such things."* It is important to note that the apostle Paul addresses this statement to brothers and sisters in Christ, or those persons who had the capability, in their human spirits, to think about such things. The capability existed because their spirits were filled with the Spirit of God, or the Holy Spirit, through a relationship with Jesus Christ.

The unregenerate person, the one who has not accepted Jesus Christ as Lord and Savior and is not walking in a vibrant relationship with him, has only the human spirit to rely on. The human spirit, which is connected only to the things of this world, is limited and cannot fathom the higher aspects of the Spirit of God. This is addressed in 1 Corinthians 2:9-11:

> *However, as it is written: "No eye has seen, no ear has heard, no mind has conceived what God has prepared for those who love him" – but God*

has revealed it to us by his Spirit. The Spirit searches all things, even the deep things of God. For who among men knows the thoughts of a man except the man's spirit within him? In the same way no one knows the thoughts of God except the Spirit of God.

It is possible to be one of the most established, competent, and literate thinkers in the world, yet still be limited because our thoughts cannot extend into the realm of the Spirit of God. This is why there are so many varied and wide interpretations of the Bible. Depending on the people you talk to, a scripture in the Bible can mean one thing, and to the other person it will mean something entirely different. This is because the word of God is not meant to be understood and interpreted merely by the thoughts of man. One must get into the mind of the Spirit, through the renewing of our natural minds, in order to understand the word of God.

Isaiah 55:8-9 confirms this by saying, *"For my thoughts are not your thoughts, neither are your ways my ways," declares the* LORD. *"As the heavens are higher than the earth, so are my ways higher than your ways and my thoughts than your thoughts."*

Ephesians 4:17-24 states:

So I tell you this, and insist on it in the Lord, that you must no longer live as the Gentiles do, in the futility of their thinking. They are darkened in their understanding and separated from the life of God because of the ignorance that is in them due to the hardening of their hearts. Having lost all sensitivity, they have given themselves over to sensuality so as to indulge in every kind of impurity, with a continual lust for more.

You, however, did not come to know Christ that way. Surely you heard of him and were taught in him in accordance with the truth that is in Jesus. You were taught, with regard to your former way of life, to put off your old self, which is being corrupted by its deceitful desires; to be made new in the attitude of your minds; and to put on the new self, created to be like God in true righteousness and holiness.

Being separated from God creates such darkness in our spirits that we can no longer realize the light of his Spirit. Our spirits, though functional from the perspective of the world, are dead. *Death* means the cessation of life. Absent from a relationship with Christ, we do not have the *life* of Christ residing in our spirits, and life without Christ is not life at all. This places us at risk of all kinds of impure thoughts, and gives Satan an opportunity to feed evil thoughts into our minds because of the lack of Holy Spirit renewal. We are urged to put off the old self — the body, soul, and spirit divorced from God — and put on the new self, which is our body, soul, and spirit under the subjection of the Holy Spirit. Only then will we realize God's potential for our lives, and walk in the personality that God created us to have.

This spiritual aspect of humanity is what separates Christians from non-Christians, and kingdom-minded people from mere churchgoers. The extent to which we subject ourselves to Holy Spirit life, instruction, and worship is the extent that our human spirits, and subsequently our bodies and souls, are informed and energized by the things of God.

It is therefore possible that a person who is an extrovert in his human spirit can become an introvert once he is subjected to the Holy Spirit. The reverse is also true. The question is, how has the Lord uniquely fashioned me, and to what extent is the Holy Spirit using my uniqueness to accomplish his purpose?

A knife is an inanimate object with a handle and a blade that is used for cutting. In the hands of a murderous spirit, that knife can be used for killing. The same knife in the hands of a chef can be used to help create delicious meals. The nature of the object is not the issue. The issue is how the object is being used — and how it is intended to be used.

For introverts who have been created to be quieter and less outgoing than their extroverted counterparts, the question is, how is God using them through the Holy Spirit? Introverts are often misunderstood, neglected, and maligned, but God can and is using them for mighty exploits within the kingdom.

Levels of Introversion

There's no such thing as a 100 percent pure introvert. All introverts are a mixture of a greater degree of introversion, along with a lesser degree of extroversion. Introverts have a "home base" of introversion. In other words, they function more out of their introverted selves than their extroverted selves. Conversely, all extroverts also have a lesser degree of introversion. This is supported by the fact that all extroverts occasionally need time to recharge their batteries and be alone as well. No extrovert wants to be around people every day, every second of the day, all the time. Introverts as well do not want to be alone all the time; they also cherish relationships with other people and can, at times, resemble extroverts.

I surprise people at my church when I tell them I am an introvert. They look at me as if my head were screwed on upside down. "*You*, an introvert?" they say incredulously. "Yeah, right." They respond this way because when I am at church, I tend to function out of my extroverted self. Whether it is counseling, preaching, teaching, or fellowship, a church such as mine that leans toward extroversion tends to draw out the extroverted side of me more so than the introverted side. But this drains me of energy, and I need to frequently recharge in relative solitude.

Many introverted pastors will probably identify with this. The demands of their calling mean that they have to be social creatures in order to meet the demands of their office. Making hospital and home visits, answering telephone calls, leading the congregation, praying openly and publicly, marketing the church, and evangelizing are all functions of an extroverted vocation that introverted pastors will perform out of their extroverted selves. But once these necessary functions are done, the introverted pastor is drained and will need to seek quiet time. Often, the effort to be extroverted will seem false, and it may affect his or her health.

Both introversion and extroversion, when extreme, can put the person at risk of being out of compliance with the Lord's desire for their lives. In the case of extroversion, people can be so outgoing and oriented toward others that they never have time to be still, meditate, and examine their own faith. They are always on the go, always running to one meeting or social engagement after another. They have no problem being with people until the wee hours of the morning—at the cost of their own rest. They have to answer every phone call, say yes to every meeting request, open the door to everyone who knocks, and accept every party invitation.

For extreme introverts, they may isolate themselves to a point that is spiritually and physically unhealthy, even bordering on *avoidant personality disorder*, a term used by psychologists to describe a disorder when a person avoids almost all social interaction because of fear of criticism or rejection. They may deny legitimate requests for fellowship, avoid social engagements they really should attend, or refuse to meet people whom they should meet. They may prefer to stay at home and watch TV rather than fellowship with believers.

Most healthy people will have a good mix of both extroversion and introversion so that they avoid the extremes of either aspect. Jesus was a good example of an extrovert and an introvert. Sometimes Jesus had to go to the mountain, away from all human contact, and pray and seek the will of the Father, refueling himself for those moments where he had to be social in order to be effective in his ministry. At other times, he was among crowds, teaching, preaching, healing those who were sick, and casting out demons with such clarity, power, and authority that it struck fear and jealousy in the hearts of the religious and political party called the Pharisees.

Whether Jesus's "home base" was introversion or extroversion, or in the center of both, is a hotly debated topic that we will not entertain here. But suffice it to say that there were so many glaring elements of both personality types in his life that it is difficult, if inadvisable, to draw such conclusions. It is enough to conclude that Jesus was a successful mixture of both, and we should be as well.

Am I Shy, an Introvert, or Both?

Shyness and introversion are often considered to be the same thing. While the two share many common traits, the fact is that shyness and introversion are not one and the same. In fact, it is possible to be an extrovert or an introvert and be shy. Conversely, you can be an introvert or an extrovert without a hint of shyness. The key to understanding this is to understand the definition of shyness.

According to the *American Heritage Dictionary*, the word "shy" comes from the Middle English word *schey*, meaning "easily frightened, or timid." This equates to the word "fear" as it is presented in several instances of scripture. There are two meanings of the word "fear" in the Bible. One is translated "piety," which means devotion or reverence. The other meaning, which is the one we are concerned with here, is "to be wary of, frightened, or timid." One of the most famous uses of the word "fear" or "timid" in the Bible is the passage in 2 Timothy 1:7:

> *For God did not give us a spirit of timidity, but a spirit of power, of love and of self-discipline.*

Paul spoke these words to his dear friend and spiritual protégé, Timothy. Immediately after these words, Paul writes, *"So do not be ashamed to testify about our Lord, or ashamed of me his prisoner"* (2 Timothy 1:8). This implies that Timothy was fearful of being bold for the Lord, and had an innate timidity that often affected his ability to minister. He likely felt frightened in intimidating social situations, or he was afraid of talking to strangers. Here, Paul had to remind him that functioning in timidity was not compatible with the purposes of God. Through the Holy Spirit, Timothy could function in power, love, and self-discipline, which are the exact opposites of fear. Where the spirit of fear is present, power, love, and self-discipline are absent. A person can never operate in the power of God, the love of God, or have self-discipline as long as the spirit of fear is present.

Interestingly enough, fear is one of the innate emotions that God gave us. All humans are afraid of *something* (anyone who says otherwise is lying or deceived). In most cases, fear is a survival mechanism that causes us to move away from perceived dangers. For instance, I will not jump into any body of water that is more than six feet deep, because I am not that good a swimmer. That fear has likely kept me from drowning.

However, when the emotion of fear evolves to the point where it hinders us from functioning according to God's will, it becomes a problem. It then becomes the *spirit of fear*. For example, one of the most common fears is public speaking. Most people think that the fear of public speaking is not an issue with ministers and preachers. I can tell you, that is a huge misconception. Many preachers are, or have been, fearful of public speaking. Yet, they press on through the fear and do what God has called them to do. Imagine how many great and anointed voices we would have been denied if these individuals had let their fears hinder them. As John Wayne once said, "Courage is being scared to death, but saddling up anyway."

As I talk with Bible-believing Christians who do not evangelize, one of the main reasons why is because of the fear of rejection. They do not want to be told that they are out of touch, that they are deluded, that they are religious nuts, etc. Because of fear of how others might perceive them, they do not share the Lord with others. Therefore, they are content with keeping silent, even though they know that so many people need an encounter with Christ. To maintain their reputations, they watch people waste away day after day in spiritual decay. Their fear of rejection overrules whatever love of God is in them.

Fear is an extremely powerful motivator. People

are often driven and directed by their fears. There are people who will not go overseas to visit loved ones because they are afraid of flying. Some sick people would rather live in pain and agony rather than risk surgery. A person who would never consider keeping a gun in his home may decide to do so because of an increase in crime in his community. Though fear can keep us safe from danger, fear also causes us to act in a manner that does not align with the will and purposes of God.

Paul's admonition to Timothy was to function in power, love, and self-discipline; not fear. Fear would cause him to avoid saying the words he needed to say to share the gospel. It would persuade him to steer clear of communities where there would be danger or where he would not be welcome. Fear would cause Timothy to be less effective, unloving, and out of control. The pangs of fear rising within him would always take precedence over the word of God.

For these reasons, the spirit of fear and its variations should not be allowed to function in a kingdom-minded Christian. It is unlikely that Timothy's timidity went away. But Timothy could function in love, transcending the timidity that was within him and placing it in subjection to the Holy Spirit.

The impact of Timothy's ability to function in love despite his timidity is clear. Timothy became one of Paul's most beloved and trusted companions. He often accompanied Paul on missionary journeys, and frequently served as Paul's ambassador. Paul could count on Timothy to be a faithful servant in the body of Christ, no matter what the situation. He was, as Proverbs 18:24 asserts, *a friend that sticketh closer than a brother (KJV)*. I know many modern pastors who would love to have at least one person like Timothy in their congregations.

Therefore, shyness and timidity make it difficult for an affected person to function in the power, love, and discipline of God because he or she may become easily frightened around people, especially strangers, or those whom the person does not know very well. It comes from the spirit of fear, which is not a product of the Holy Spirit and is not an element of God's character. But Timothy was able to function as a powerful apprentice in the kingdom of God despite his shyness, with the Holy Spirit's help.

Introversion, on the other hand, has no basis in fear. While both shy people and introverts often withdraw from people, shy people do so out of *fear*. Introverts do so out of *preference*. Introverts prefer quieter, solitary activities, or gatherings with just a few close friends, and are not energized by situations that involve many people. They are not as likely to be the life of the party, and are known to be quiet, especially around people that they do not know. Introverts can be shy or non-shy. Those who are non-shy can be just as bold at preaching the gospel, or introducing themselves to strangers, or giving speeches as those who are shy. It's just not something that they thrive at doing, whereby the extrovert clearly thrives on these types of social interactions.

So, since both shy people and introverts both withdraw from people to an extent, how can God be glorified with either of these personality traits? After all, to be a biblically based, kingdom- minded Christian is to deal with people, worship with believers, minister to those in need, be ministered to by members of the flock, and build vital relationships within the body of Christ. Can any discourse about withdrawing from people be compatible with kingdom theology, which is so utterly comprised of binding believers together in vital relationships? And we understand that shyness is not something that people should acquiesce to, because any spirit based in fear counteracts the love of God. They should always challenge the spirit of fear by subjecting it to the Holy Spirit, and by allowing the Spirit to take control of their lives.

Introverts, however, have traits that are biblical and can be used by God for the furtherance of his kingdom and for building powerful relationships in the body of Christ. So let's look more closely at the personality of an introvert and exactly what it means to be an introverted person in the kingdom of God.

True Picture of an Introvert

Apart from physical rest, most people have things that they like to do to "unwind," "recharge their batteries," or "blow off steam." Extroverts typically enjoy activities that feature a high level of social interaction. Nightclubs, parties, and bar happy hours are often replete with extroverts.

Church gatherings are also havens for extroverts. The purposes of a church gathering are to foster fellowship, to interact with fellow believers, to worship and pray together, to gather and give strength, encouragement, and exhortation. The energy received from fellow believers make a church gathering what it is. Extroverts, who receive their energy from others, thrive in this type of environment.

Introverts thrive on time spent in quieter or more solitary activities. A typical introvert enjoys time praying alone or with a few friends in a group setting. He or she may enjoy listening to music more on an iPod than in a concert hall with hundreds of thousands of people around. Time spent at home reading the Bible is likely to be more beneficial to an introvert than a Bible study involving several people.

Being an introvert does not mean being a hermit. Hermits completely remove themselves from human interaction. Hermits are common in certain Catholic orders where people withdraw themselves from society out of religious conviction. However, introverts are all around us, every day. They attend church with us, they work with us, and they are in the marketplace. They attend parties, go to restaurants, attend the theater, and participate in clubs and groups. The idea that introverts do not like people is false.

They just prefer the quieter moments in their lives as opposed to those where there are a lot of people milling around. The moments when they unwind or recharge their batteries are likely to be during their quieter, more introspective moments.

The word *introvert* is derived from two Latin words, *intro* and *vertere*. *Intro* means "inward," and *vertere* means "turn to." Introversion is a personality type characterized by turning one's energy primarily to the self. According to Dictionary.com, an *introvert* is "a person characterized by concern primarily with his or her own thoughts and feelings," as opposed to an *extrovert*—"a person concerned primarily with the physical and social environment."

At first glance, it may appear that the extrovert is more in keeping with kingdom ministry and dynamics. After all, as kingdom believers, we are called to reach out to what is going on around us. But the introvert, with his attention primarily inward, is also biblically in line, because any change that God wants to affect in the world around us has to start inside of *us*. We have to be introspective and examine ourselves and see what God wants to change inside us.

My personal walk with the Lord has convinced me of one thing: God desires to work on me first and change me, and from the outworking of his grace in my life I can minister and reach out to others. The old Christmas song by Jill Jackson Miller, "Let There Be Peace on Earth," contains the lyric, "and let it begin with me." If I want peace to happen on earth, there must first be peace inside me. So, God can use a person who thrives on inward reflection as well as a person who thrives on the environment around him.

With the introvert's focus inward, he or she is likely to excel at activities that are more pensive in nature. Reading, watching TV or movies, studying, researching, writing, spending time on the computer, painting, drawing, or solving puzzles is typically how the introvert likes to spend most of his or her spare time. He or she typically likes to do these activities alone, or with a friend or two. Outdoor activities such as fishing, jogging, and bicycle riding, might also interest him or her. When with friends, she usually prefers conversation that is meaningful and deep, but short-lived. He does not like long meetings, and staying in church for more than a couple of hours drains him. He rarely initiates a social encounter. She will not call to invite you to dinner or to the movies, but will readily go if asked. She does not call on the phone unless there is a specific purpose to it. It is rare that an introvert will have long conversations in person or on the phone unless it is highly important, or it is a conversation with a close, dear friend or relative.

In the next chapter, we will look at the qualities of an introvert and how they line up with the word of God.

Eleven Biblical Qualities of an Introvert

In this section we will examine the qualities that define introverts and how those qualities relate to the word of God. These qualities are derived from my own experiences, and from psychological definitions of introversion. While I may use these psychological definitions, I will not interpret these definitions through the lens of psychology. I will go into the wealth of knowledge in the word of God to interpret these definitions according to scripture and help the reader see that introversion, while traditionally a psychological concept, is actually a collection of qualities that God places in select humans, and that psychology is man's attempt to study what God has already done in the *psūchê* (psyche).

Quality #1: Introverts are quiet.

I can't begin to count the number of times I have heard said of me, "Oh, he's so quiet." It is not that I do not have anything to say. It's just that I do not have as much to say as others. When I speak, I am usually direct and to the point, rarely embellishing my words with fluff and needless information. When delivering a sermon, I am not usually as long-winded as other ministers in my circle (although there have been a few exceptions). I am not one to start a conversation, and I am not big on arguments. I enjoy conversations, but just not *long* ones.

As a minister, I am surrounded by people who can talk on the telephone for hours at a time. When they meet together in fellowship, they can talk for several hours. At times, I wish I had the ability to maintain a conversation for that long. But for me, after a conversation of about one to one and a half hours (shorter or longer, depending on the subject and my interest level in it), I am looking for the exit. I simply do not have the energy to maintain a conversation for several hours.

This may make introverts seem aloof, disinterested, and unattached. This quality of silence makes many people uncomfortable, especially those who are accustomed to the more talkative, extroverted personality. On the other hand, what they do not provide in terms of raw jibber-jabber, they make up for in listening ability. According to a December 2010 article in the *Harvard Business Review*, "introverted leaders tend to listen more carefully and show greater receptivity to suggestions, making them more effective leaders of vocal teams."[11]

Introverts, because of their preference to process things internally, are often much better listeners than their extroverted counterparts. Because of their sensitive natures, they tend to have more empathy and compassion and can identify with what people are saying. They have no motivations to speak just to be heard, so they are more likely to be quiet and process what others have to say. They are more likely to take some time and think about what others have said rather than respond immediately.

As an introvert, I realized long ago that I have that listening ability. For that reason, I seem to attract people who want and need to be listened to. In American society, this seems to be a lost trait. I can't tell you how many times I have spoken to someone about an issue I am having, only to have them start talking and responding before I have finished what I had to say. And when they speak, often they are not addressing anything that I have told them. Nowadays, there is the dynamic of distracted listening, where people are trying to listen while typing on a computer, answering cell phone calls, or trying to feed hungry children. In the not-so-distant past, a

---

11   **Adam M. Grant, Francesca Gino, David A. Hofmann.** "The Hidden Advantages of Quiet Bosses" (*Harvard Business Review*, December 2010).

person could schedule a meeting with someone else and get that person's undivided attention during the meeting. Now, the meeting is likely to be interrupted by a cell phone call, a text, or a tweet that has to be answered immediately. In this multitasking, fast-paced society, the art and gift of listening seems to be sorely lacking.

The Bible presents the ability to listen as a valued trait, and holds the person who is slow of tongue in great esteem. Proverbs 10:19 states, *"When words are many, sin is not absent, but he who holds his tongue is wise."* James 1:19 says, *"My dear brothers, take note of this: Everyone should be quick to listen, slow to speak and slow to become angry."*

In Ecclesiastes 9:13-17, Qoheleth makes an interesting statement:

> *I also saw under the sun this example of wisdom that greatly impressed me: There was once a small city with only a few people in it. And a powerful king came against it, surrounded it and built huge siegeworks against it. Now there lived in that city a man poor but wise, and he saved the city by his wisdom. But nobody remembered that poor man. So I said, "Wisdom is better than strength." But the poor man's wisdom is despised, and his words are no longer heeded.*
> *The quiet words of the wise are more to be heeded than the shouts of a ruler of fools."*

This scripture appears to juxtapose the methods of a king who is powerful and brash against those of a humble but quiet man. It was through the quiet, humble man's wisdom that the city was saved. However, because he was not a man of power and position, and because he did not attract attention to himself, his words were despised and not given further attention — even though his wisdom saved the city.

How often in our society are those who are verbal, outgoing, and aggressive preferred over those who are quiet and unassuming? How often is wisdom sought from a quiet, meek person as opposed to one who shows up at all the right places and says all the right things? Extroversion is often seen as a strong personality trait, while introversion is seen as weak and ineffective. However, this scripture vindicates those with wisdom who are quiet and humble by saying that the quiet words of the wise should be given more attention than the shouts of a ruler of fools. While the central theme of this scripture is wisdom versus folly, an important, secondary issue is how one's status or position affects our willingness to hear. We are more willing to hear those who are powerful rather than those are quiet and wise. Introverts are quiet, but many have great wisdom and much to offer — if people take the time to get to know them.

Jesus notes in Matthew 6:5-8:

"And when you pray, do not be like the hypo-

crites, for they love to pray standing in the syn-agogues and on the street corners to be seen by men. I tell you the truth, they have received their reward in full. But when you pray, go into your room, close the door and pray to your Father, who is unseen. Then your Father, who sees what is done in secret, will reward you. And when you pray, do not keep on babbling like pagans, ***for they think they will be heard because of their many words.*** *Do not be like them, for your Father knows what you need before you ask him."*

It is interesting that even in biblical times, the people who had the most to say — and didn't mind saying it — were the ones who were most valued, respected, and honored. The hypocrites and pagans in Jesus's time knew this, and would try to win the approval of others by praying in public, and by using as many words as possible in order to impress others. But this phenomenon is not just limited to biblical times. Even in this modern day, you have spiritual "show-offs" who love to stand up in the middle of the congregation or in the pulpit and recite loud and long prayers in order to show people how spiritual and anointed they are. In fact, in many of my circles, the longer the prayer, the more "approved" it appears to be.

Does God really require so many words? For instance, if I am having a financial problem, isn't it just as effective to simply say, "Lord, bless and heal my finances" as it is to pray for twenty minutes? The latter may be a better show, and may evenpurport to demonstrate a greater level of compassion and concern. But a quick prayer to the Lord is just as effective to his ears as a long one and may be more effective, particularly if the long prayer is delivered just to impress people. The Lord knows just what we need even before we ask him. A long prayer is not going to give him any more information than he already has[12].

The quiet persona is just as important to the Lord as a vociferous one. Rather than try to make introverts more active in speaking, we should respect their quiet natures and realize that they have much to offer because of — not in spite of — their quietness.

Quality #2: Introverts enjoy solitude.

Introverts are energized by time spent alone, or in the company of just a few close friends. Parties or other social gatherings where there are many people tend to drain them if they attend for too long. Church meetings, which are typically the primary

---

12   I make a distinction here between people who pray long just to impress others, versus people who pray long because they are passionate about the subject of their prayer, or because they are deeply troubled about something. Luke 6:12 recounts an instance of Jesus praying all night to God.

social gatherings for kingdom-minded Christians, can also be draining if they go on for too long.

For the introvert who enjoys spending time alone, how can this be reconciled with the fact that God encourages the saints to get together in fellowship? As Christians, we are called to build relationships in the body of Christ. How can that be done if we are alone all the time? Furthermore, how does this work out for introverts who have roommates? What about those who are married and have families?

Let's abolish one stereotype. Introverts are not hermits or social misfits. The typical introvert does not live in a cottage somewhere deep in the woods in unsettled territory. Many introverts are married, have families, and are involved in their churches and communities. They have jobs ranging from janitors to officials in the White House, to actors and movie directors. Introverts are in the congregation as well as behind the pulpit.

I love and enjoy spending time with my family and the people in my church. I look forward to those moments and cherish them. I just need more moments of quiet time to refresh and energize myself. This is not being antisocial. In comparison, I love food. I just don't eat as much as some people. That doesn't make me *anti-food*. I just don't have that big of an appetite.

Jesus was undoubtedly a busy man. Beginning his ministry at the age of thirty, he spent a great deal of time teaching and preaching, casting out demons, healing the sick, and dealing with crowds. The pressures and demands on his time were overwhelming, and there is no doubt, based on an exhaustive reading of the Gospels, that Jesus enjoyed ministering to people. However, there were many times that he needed to "recharge his batteries," and he would often seek solitary places to pray and spend time with the Lord.

In the beginning of his ministry, Jesus was led by the Spirit into the desert (Luke 4:1). In Luke 4:42, Jesus went to a solitary place to pray. In Luke 5:15-16, we read that Jesus often went to lonely places and prayed. Jesus went to the mountainside to pray (Luke 6:12). In one instance, he took Peter, James, and John with him (Luke 9:28). Matthew 14:13 says that Jesus withdrew by boat to a solitary place.

While Christian introverts will certainly use their alone time to pray and seek the presence of God, they will also use this time to engage in other sedentary indoor activities such as reading, writing, composing, drawing, painting, and watching TV, or outdoor endeavors such as bicycle riding, jogging, fishing, or building. Their choice of activities will typically involve minimal involvement with other people, unless they are close friends. Their alone time allows them moments to engage in their naturally creative abilities. Their friendships are few, but of such endearing quality that one close friend to an introvert can be the same as fifteen superficial friends to an extrovert.

Relationships with spouses and immediate family are not as draining to introverts as other relationships. These relationships typically have strong elements of trust and understanding. Being with spouses, family, or even close friends does not have the same dynamic as being in a social situation with acquaintances or strangers. There is no pressure to say the right thing, or look the right way, or impress anyone (not that introverts are *that* concerned about impressing anyone). With spouses, family, and close friends, introverts can relax and allow themselves time to recharge.

It is my prayer that the Christian introvert who reads this book will realize an important benefit of our personality. As introverts, we enjoy spending time alone. We recharge in solitude. This presents many wondrous opportunities to draw closer to God and spend time communing with him. Many people struggle to find quiet time to spend with God. But most introverts can use their planned time alone to read the Word, pray, worship, or just to "be still, and know that I am God" (Psalm 46:10). To the Christian introvert, Christ is the best friend we could ever have, more so than any of our earthly friends. If we enjoy spending time with them, how much more should we enjoy spending time with our heavenly friend, Jesus Christ? As an introvert who is blessed to have many moments of solitude in my life, I have no excuse to fall short on my personal devotion to God. The Christian introvert has an opportunity to build a powerful relationship with God born of the moments, hours, and days spent alone with him.

An article in *Christianity Today* profiles a woman who has been instrumental in bringing healing, hope, and love to many poor and forgotten people in Mozambique. The article mentions that there are "credible reports that Heidi Baker heals the deaf and raises the dead." She is known worldwide for healing miracles, and spends a third of the year on the charismatic preaching circuit. She leads a church association of ten thousand congregations, and she, along with her husband, has a passion to bring the gospel to places where many Christians fear to tread. She also has a gift for making friends. Sounds like an extrovert, right?

Actually, the article quotes her husband, Rolland Baker, as saying that Heidi is "fundamentally an introvert, longing for hours alone in prayer and meditation."[13]

I believe these times alone are crucial for her to be able to meet the demands of such a busy and vital ministry.

Deny the introvert his or her natural time alone, and you may be denying the kingdom of God the benefits of what the introvert can offer that is sparked by time alone. Solitude is a biblical concept that is a blessing to the introvert, as long as the introvert does not take it to the extreme and reject the equal blessing of having good Christian relationships.

---

13   Tim Stafford ,"Miracles in Mozambique," *Christianity Today*, (vol 6, No. 12), May 2012.

Quality #3: The friends of an introvert are few, but quality.

Proverbs 18:24 states, *"A man that hath friends must shew himself friendly: and there is a friend that sticketh closer than a brother"* (*KJV*).

In this Facebook generation, people take pride in the number of friends they have. I once saw a TV commercial where a young girl is sitting in front of her laptop bragging about the hundreds of friends she has on Facebook, yet decrying the mere nineteen friends that her parents have. Meanwhile, another shot shows her parents with a few friends out riding bicycles and enjoying their lives spent in the great outdoors.

I identify more with the parents. I would rather have a few friends and spend quality one-on-one time with them, rather than have hundreds of friends whom I may not know on a social networking site.

Many introverts do not take pleasure in having a lot of friends. In fact, *too* many friends are draining to them. Introverts like a few quality relationships and invest themselves heavily in those relationships. Their friends tend to be introverts like themselves. Their basic definition of *friend* is someone whom they have spent quality one-on-one time with, trust him or her implicitly, know an extensive amount of information about him or her, and have a lifestyle that is compatible with their own. Their idea of a friend is someone with whom they have *fellowship*. We well discuss this shortly. Their friends tend to be few primarily because of the next quality.

Quality #4: Introverts choose friends carefully.

Because of their quiet, solitary natures, introverts normally do not attract many friends and may have difficulty with establishing romantic relationships. I remember a conversation I had with a fellow introvert, and he shared with me how he started to build a friendship with a young lady who was a member of his church choir. Though Warren and Jackie were only friends, their conversations hinted that there might be romantic possibilities on the horizon. They had been out to dinner and to the movies together many times, and Warren finally decided that Jackie was the perfect woman for him and asked her on an official date. Jackie quickly accepted his invitation, and Warren, for the first time in several years, was dating again.

He decided to keep his date low-key and simple—dinner at an Italian restaurant, and a movie. But Jackie wanted to do something different. The dinner was fine, but Jackie wanted to go to a secular nightclub for dancing afterward. Warren, not much for the nightclub scene, wasn't receptive to the idea, but Jackie tried to legitimize it by mentioning that a popular Christian act would be performing there. Warren was not going for it. He preferred something a little less gregarious than hanging around a bunch of loud teenagers and some even louder adults. Jackie finally acquiesced, and the two went on their first of many dates over a six-month period.

Warren had grown quite fond of Jackie in the few months that they were dating, and he was excited that the relationship had the blessing of his pastor. Though it was a little premature to start making marriage plans, Warren was certain that Jackie would eventually become his wife.

Only two months later, Warren came to Sunday services and noticed Jackie sitting in the congregation beside a man who had developed a reputation in the church as a "bad boy." A "bad boy" is a man who walks around with lots of swagger, flaunts his masculinity, caters to himself and himself only, and generally believes he is the greatest gift God ever gave to women. Jackie and the bad boy appeared to be quite chummy, whispering to one another during the service. Warren, who was a member of the men's choir and was sitting in the choir loft, shot frequent glances at them from behind the pulpit.

When the service was over, Jackie hurried to Warren and greeted him as she usually did. They made arrangements to spend the rest of that Sunday at her parents' house. Warren made no mention of his brooding jealousy over the attention she was giving the bad boy, who was whispering *who knew what* into

Jackie's ear.

The next Monday, Warren came home from work at around 6:00 p.m. and tried to call Jackie. No answer. He called again an hour later. Still no answer. It wasn't unusual for Jackie to be out of touch for two hours or slightly more. But when he couldn't reach her after three hours, he began to get worried.

His initial inclination was to go over to her house and see what was wrong. But he decided against it. He wanted Jackie to know that he trusted her. And he did. At least he thought he did.

Finally, at 11:00 that night, he was able to reach Jackie. Jackie explained that she was tired when she arrived home from work, fell asleep, and didn't hear the phone ring. She said she would call him the next morning. Jackie had never lied to him, so Warren had no reason to believe she was lying now.

The next morning, Jackie called Warren and told him that she was going to spend the day with her parents. She told him that she would call him as soon as she left her parents' home. Warren was okay with this. After all, she had never lied to him, and although he had a strong urge to see her, he didn't want to hinder or disrespect Jackie's relationship with her parents. Warren settled down for a day of TV watching and waited for Jackie to call.

At 7:00 p.m., Jackie hadn't called. Surely she had left her parents' home by now. He called her on her cell phone. The call went directly to voice mail. Several unanswered calls and three hours later, Warren heard a knock at his door. It was Jackie. He was initially excited to see her, but quickly toned down his excitement when he noticed the serious look on her face as he allowed her inside his apartment.

"I have to talk to you," Jackie said.

Warren nodded and listened intently, wondering what was bothering her. Jackie didn't bother to remove her jacket, which meant she had no plans to stay. That was the first sign that something was awry.

Jackie, with the softest and most unassuming of voices, said, "I don't think we should see each other anymore."

Warren's spirits deflated quickly and painfully. When he tried to determine why Jackie no longer wanted a relationship with him, Jackie responded, "It's not you. It's me. I don't think I'm ready for this type of relationship."

"What type of relationship are you ready for?" Warren wondered aloud, but Jackie never answered him. She said she had to go. Then, just as quickly and as suddenly as she arrived, she walked out of his apartment.

Not wanting to lose her, Warren put on his shoes and grabbed a jacket from his closet. He then ran out the door and, realizing that Jackie had already boarded the elevator, made his way to the stairs. There was only one flight of stairs to the lobby, and as Warren flung open the stairway lobby door and hurried to the entrance, he saw Jackie, who had already left the building, climbing in the passenger seat of a Toyota Camry driven by none other than the church bad boy.

Warren stood there for a minute, in shock, as he started to process what would become one of the most painful moments of his life.

In retrospect, Warren believes his introversion caused the breakup of his relationship. He believes that Jackie could not handle his quiet nature and wanted to date someone who was more outgoing and adventurous. He decries how unjust it is that a woman would break up with a man who would take good care of her, and start dating a man who would do nothing but use her and abuse her. He laments on being single while so many gregarious, and often abusive, men manage to attract so many good women.

Some women mistakenly associate introversion with weakness, boredom, and disinterest, and extroverts with strength, vitality, and excitement. This leads many women to be initially attracted to extroverts more so than introverts. Introverts are not a great sell in this fast-paced society we live in. One of the disadvantages of being an introvert is the possibility of limited prospects for romance. It's like being the wallflower at the party who is never invited to dance.

In a society that values extroverts, introverts are not likely to have a lot of people beating down the door to be friends with them. But when a person seems to be encroaching on or desiring a friendship with an introvert, they are slow to open up and may be distrustful at first. This is because introverts can be highly analytical at times. Every person, whether introvert or extrovert, wants good friends — people they can get along with and would be compatible with. Introverts will take the time to analyze a person to determine if the person is a good match as a friend.

Proverbs 13:20 states, *"He who walks with the wise grows wise, but a companion of fools suffers harm."* This little pearl of wisdom shows the importance of being selective in one's choice of friends. The old saying, "If you hang around dogs, you're going to get fleas" applies here. You are often defined by and affected by the type of people you select to be a part of your life. And those people reflect your views, your sensibilities, and your outlook on life.

I have met many parents who have raised teenagers and remember lovingly the days when their children were devoted to them. Then all of a sudden, they started hanging with the wrong group of friends, and everything changed. That sweet child had suddenly become a rabble-rouser. The studious brainiac with all As had started skipping classes and acting out in school. A child who would never argue with her parents suddenly wages war against them. For the Christian who wants to remain faithful to the Lord, her friends are a crucial part of the equation.

Consider this scripture:

Do not make friends with a hot-tempered man,
do not associate with one easily angered, or you
may learn his ways and get yourself ensnared
(Proverbs 22:24-25).

It is clear from Solomon's pearls of wisdom that choosing the right friends can be a blessing to you, and choosing the wrong friends can lead you down a path of destruction. The introvert's tendency to carefully choose friends aligns with the scriptural admonition to be careful whom we associate with.

This doesn't mean that all introverts choose the right friends all the time. Introverts can choose wrong friends just like anyone else. But with the aid of the Holy Spirit, this aspect of our personality can be fine-tuned to separate the wheat from the chaff.

In 2 Corinthians 6:14, Paul says, *"Do not be yoked together with unbelievers. For what do righteousness and wickedness have in common? Or what fellowship can light have with darkness?"* Many people think this scripture applies only to marriages and potential marriages. But I believe this scripture applies to all relationships in the body of Christ. Further, it states:

What harmony is there between Christ and Belial? What does a believer have in common with an unbeliever? What agreement is there between the temple of God and idols? For we are the temple of the living God. As God has said: "I will

*live with them and walk among them, and I will
be their God, and they will be my people."
"Therefore come out from them and be separate,
says the Lord. Touch no unclean thing, and I
will receive you."
"I will be a Father to you, and you will be my
sons and daughters, says the Lord Almighty." (2
Corinthians 6:15-18)*

This scripture demands that Christians be dis-
criminating in selecting the people with whom they
fellowship, and the deciding factor is whether or not
they are believers in Christ. For the Christian, any
person whom he calls a friend and has a deep relationship rooted in fellowship should also have a relationship with Christ. God does not call us to fellowship with unbelievers.

This raises a question: if we are called to be friends
only with believers, how are we to minister to unbelievers? Don't we need to be friends with unsaved
people in order to have an opportunity to minister
to them?

Let me make a distinction between the word *friend*
and the word *fellowship*. The scripture in 2 Corinthians 6:14 never mentions the word *friend*, but mentions *fellowship*. A closer look at this word reveals
something shocking, yet appropriate. The Greek
word represented by *fellowship* in 2 Corinthians
means *intercourse*. We know the word intercourse
from the term *sexual intercourse*. It speaks of an inti-

macy, a participation in the affairs of another, a joining together. The scripture in 2 Corinthians 6:14 does
not tell us not to have *friendships* with unbelievers. It
tells us not to have *fellowship* with unbelievers. As an
introvert, I tend to seek fellowship over mere friendship.

Friendship can range in level from mere acquain-
tance to the deep, intimate friendship that is evident
in a marriage. Two people can consider one another
friends if they see each other only once or twice per
year. Intimacy and frequency of contact may vary
with friendships. In this social networking age, people have online friends they've never personally met.

Fellowship is a more intimate form of friendship.
The Bible cautions us against the more intimate form
of friendship with unbelievers where we have intercourse with them, sexual or otherwise. It warns us
against mutual participation in the affairs of unbelievers. We are not to become so joined with unbelievers that we inwardly start to look just like them.

However, friendships with unbelievers that do
not ascend to an intimate level can be used to effectively minister to them the gospel of Jesus Christ.

Quality #5: Introverts examine themselves.

> *Examine yourselves to see whether you are in
> the faith; test yourselves. Do you not realize that
> Christ Jesus is in you — unless, of course, you*

fail the test? (2 Corinthians 13:5).

This is a controversial passage that can lead one to selfish introspection if not careful. The danger for introverts, who are prone to inward mental energy, is to make a laundry list of sins and flaws that we must fix, and then make ourselves a project to work on so that we move toward perfection.

What is wrong with that? Does the Lord not want us to better ourselves? Of course. Should we be aware of sins and flaws in our lives? Definitely. The issue is the extent to which we examine ourselves. Although this can be a dangerous area for introverts, it can also be a great benefit if our mental energy is directed in the right manner.

Let me put this in greater clarity. For a number of years I operated a post-prison ministry, which involved counseling men and women who were preparing to be released from prison into society. Being released is a daunting reality for many former prisoners. Many of them have not lived outside of prison for many years and need to adjust to the nuances of the outside world. Many of them have no income, no place to live, and no other resources to assist them upon release. Because of their status as former prisoners, it is difficult for them to get jobs that would pay anything close to a living wage. Many of them are released into neighborhoods replete with drugs, violence, and poverty — the same temptations that landed them in prison in the first place. The challenges were so discouraging that one of my goals for each person I counseled was to get them to see that they needed Jesus Christ in their lives in order to have any chance at success upon release.

I met one man, whom I will call "Isley." Isley initially seemed to be the poster child for successful post-prison reintegration. He had accepted Christ in his life before release, and he was excited about his newfound relationship with the Lord and his possibilities upon release. I met him several weeks after his release, when he was referred to a transitional house for ex-prisoners that a team from my church and I operated. The house provided round-the-clock shelter and support services to men recently released from prison, and provided a safe, redemptive, Christian environment where they could begin the process of reentry.

Isley moved into the house and set up weekly counseling sessions with me. I quickly discovered during our first counseling session that he didn't attend church on a regular basis. His job at a department store required him to work on Sundays, but it was clear there were other motivations. He rarely read the Bible, never prayed, and steered clear of other church meetings that were more compatible with his schedule.

When I pressed him further on this, he admitted that he attended church when he was first released, but stopped going after a couple of Sundays. When I asked him why, he made a statement that is not unusual among the population of men and women who have been incarcerated. He replied, "I am not good enough to go to church."

What caused him to make such a statement? In the next session, we looked at this further. After some questioning, Isley revealed that the constant preaching and teaching about sin, and the seemingly self-righteous attitude of some of the congregation members, left him feeling as if he wasn't good enough to attend church, and so he stopped going. The preaching and teaching caused him to look at his own life and realize how truly sinful he was. His struggles with sexual temptation, cursing, cigarette smoking, and his anger issues left him feeling as if he would never measure up in his church community. Part of it was also his ingrained beliefs, likely present from childhood, that in order to be in church, you have to be free from sin.

I understand Isley's struggle. Many people have sin in their lives, but have been told, either directly or indirectly, that they have to be perfect in order to attend church or have a relationship with Jesus. Nothing could be further from the truth.

1 John 2:1 states, *"My little children, these things write I unto you, that ye sin not. And if any man sin, we have an advocate with the Father, Jesus Christ the righteous (KJV)."* It is true that the word of God helps us achieve victory over sinful behavior and sinful thoughts. It is true that God desires us to be free from the vices of the enemy. No person reading this book,

and certainly not the person writing it, is free from sin. My pastor, Paul Gaskins, says several times in his sermons that if anyone ever presented his sins on a movie screen in front of an audience, he would not be able to look at them. He would have to run away in shame.

The danger in turning the microscope on ourselves, as 2 Corinthians 13:5 seems to say, is that we will discover so many inadequacies that we will either get discouraged and fall away from the faith, as Isley did, or we will start a process of trying to fix ourselves, which will lead to frustration and utter failure. But the second half of 1 John 2:1 is extremely vital. *"And if any man sin, we have an **advocate** with the Father, Jesus Christ the righteous."* An advocate is one that speaks for us and pleads our case. Jesus Christ intercedes for us, speaking for us with the Father. When we establish a relationship with Jesus, he becomes our righteousness. Without him, we are still wallowing in our sins and iniquities.

Let's look at 2 Corinthians 13:5 again. It states, *"Examine yourselves to see whether you are in the faith."* While it is important to be aware of sin in our lives that may hinder our potential, the scripture is not saying that we should develop a laundry list of our sins. We will never like what we see. Instead, we should examine ourselves to see if we are in the faith; in other words, we should make sure that our faith in Jesus Christ is steadfast and secure. The inner-directed mental energy that is a natural aspect of introversion can be used to further build our relationship with Jesus Christ by always looking to see if we are in the faith and working on building a more vibrant relationship with Jesus.

We can never fix ourselves, but Jesus, to the extent that we remain connected with him in faith, can fix any sin and malady in our lives. As we continue to praise him, worship him, pray, and stay connected with other like-minded Christians, the Holy Spirit will constantly be working on us, showing us ourselves, helping us to pray, making us more like Jesus, and bringing us into the place where God desires us to be. The focus should never be on our imperfections, but on Jesus Christ and his righteousness.

To introverts who are naturally thoughtful and introspective, examining Jesus within us is scriptural and will lead to a more fruitful relationship with him.

A song that we sing in church, with lyrics from the following psalm, helps us to remember how important it is for us that Jesus Christ is our hope:

> *Why are you downcast, O my soul?*
> *Why so disturbed within me?*
> *Put your hope in God, for I will yet praise him,*
> *my Savior and my God (Psalm 42:5).*

Quality #6: Introverts do not like to draw attention

to themselves.

*Humble yourselves in the sight of the Lord,
and he shall lift you up (James 4:10, KJV).*

Many people assume that introverts are shy. While it is true that some are, many are not shy, but simply prefer not to draw too much attention to themselves. They are known for doing things for people without expecting much in return (a simple "thank you" will usually do the trick). Since they do not draw much energy from outside themselves, particularly people around them, they are less likely to try to impress others. They do not like the limelight, and are perfectly happy working behind the scenes on many endeavors.

There are those whose self-worth is determined by the praise and approbation of others. To them, they feel good about themselves when they are rewarded or approved of by other people. As an introvert, my energy does not come from others, but comes from within. As a result, my self-worth does not depend on things or people outside myself.

Don't get me wrong. I like to be praised and thanked and appreciated just like anyone else. I like the good feeling I get when someone says I have done something nice, or done a good job, or helped him or her in a crucial area of life. A certain level of attention from others is always good and always nice to experience. However, as an introvert, I don't thrive on it.

As a result, even if no one tells me I am a good person, or no one tells me I have done a good job, or no one seems to appreciate what I do, it may spur a limited amount of self-examination (after all, if no one tells me I am doing a good job, or that I am a good person, maybe I am *not*). But it does not degrade my self-worth, nor will it necessarily affect my efforts to continue doing what I have been doing.

Scientists believe that a brain hormone called dopamine is responsible for feelings of reward, attention, and self-worth. Studies show that introverts have less activity in that area of the brain than in other areas, as opposed to extroverts. Therefore, while introverts certainly like praise and appreciation, they require less of it than extroverts. As a result, they do not constantly have to be "massaged" by others in order to feel as if they matter in this world.

My own experiences reflect this truth. Whenever I do nice things for people, a "thank you" is usually sufficient for me, and I do not need much beyond that. Even if I do not get any appreciation whatsoever, I will still do it again in a heartbeat. In fact, I will likely get annoyed if I receive *too* much praise for something. I recognize that I may not be perfect, but I also recognize that God has put me on this earth for a purpose, and that I am worth something to God as long as I am moving into my kingdom purpose. I do not need others to define my self-worth for me. If someone calls me a name, it may sting for a moment, but it is not going to change who I am. Though the enemy constantly tries to bring my weaknesses to the forefront, or amplify my failures, I do not dwell on them. Instead, I dwell on Jesus and receive my self-worth from the light of the Holy Spirit that resides within me.

Even when it comes to my style of dress, I prefer to wear clothing that is sharp and well fashioned, but that does not draw undue attention to myself. I will not be caught dead wearing a yellow suit, walking around in feather boas, or riding around in some trendy and ostentatious vehicle. I will not wear anything that detracts from the holiness within me, no matter if it is in style or not (I can't begin to tell you how many young men and women I have counseled on this point—on their preference to wear provocative, revealing, and often foolish-looking clothing simply because it is in style). I will not tailor my dressing style in order to win approval.

Because I possess many skills that are useful in my home and in my ministry, I have been told that I am a jack-of-all-trades. While I acknowledge that I possess those skills, I do not advertise them or make a big deal about them. I prefer to keep them to myself unless a need arises that I can address using one of my skills. I do not go around wearing a sign that says, "I am Louis Jones, and I can do anything." Most of my friends know about these skills only because they have seen me use them—not because I have talked about them.

Matthew 6:1-4 (NKJV) warns against seeking the

approbation of people for the things that we do:

> *Take heed that you do not do your charitable deeds before men, to be seen by them. Otherwise you have no reward from your Father in heaven. Therefore, when you do a charitable deed, do not sound a trumpet before you as the hypocrites do in the synagogues and in the streets, that they may have glory from men. Assuredly, I say to you, they have their reward. But when you do a charitable deed, do not let your left hand know what your right hand is doing, that your charitable deed may be in secret; and your Father who sees in secret will Himself reward you openly.*

Isn't this a far cry away from the current penchant of advertising all of the good things that we do? The scripture implies that there are two types of rewards; those that come from men, and those that come from God. When we do our good deeds to be seen by men, our reward comes from men. This is a compelling lesson to those who flood the airwaves and the TV channels with their good works, hoping to raise money. And they may be successful at raising money, but they only have glory from people. But for those who do their good deeds, are not motivated by the approval of people, and do their deeds even if no one sees or appreciates them, then God's promise in Matthew is that he will reward us openly. In other words, God's blessings on our lives will be clear and apparent to us — and anyone who relates to us.

Can an introvert be boastful and arrogant, drawing attention to himself? It is possible, just as it is possible for the extrovert to be humble and to conduct his affairs without being driven by the approval of others. However, the typical introvert in Christ is primed to be predisposed to the Holy Spirit's leading, and will be receptive to the scriptural mandate that we reserve praise and glory for God, and not for ourselves.

> *They utter speech, and speak insolent things;*
> *All the workers of iniquity boast in themselves*
> *(Psalm 94:4, NKJV).*

Quality #7: Introverts are thoughtful and reflective.

> *"Come now, let us reason together," says the*
> *LORD (Isaiah 1:18).*
> *Reflect on what I am saying, for the Lord will*
> *give you insight into all this (2 Timothy 2:7).*

Introverts love to think, reason, and reflect. We are not just surface-level thinkers; we think *deeply*. We are prone to being analytical. We are rarely impulsive and reckless, because we usually like to think about things before we act on them. We consider our actions carefully. We do not answer questions or solve problems quickly, unless we have had an opportunity to think about them. In a dispute, we are most likely to consider both sides carefully before making a decision.

The Word of God has much to say about our thought processes, and I could easily devote the entirety of this book to discussion of those processes. But I trust that a few scriptures will establish the premise that God wants us to think well, and think often. This quality about introverts works well in those who seek a deeper relationship with God. Because introverts are prone to thinking on a deeper level, introverts are poised to go beyond mere surface-level knowledge of God and explore him with careful study and detail. We are less likely to be influenced in our thoughts by things external to ourselves.

My own life serves as a testimony. When I first became a Christian during my teen years, I was among Christians who prided themselves in pointing out sin in almost every instance, and emphasizing how the devil was at work in that situation. One of the things that influenced me to go to church was a talk with a friend who spent several minutes telling me about hellfire and brimstone and how I would go to hell if I didn't accept Christ into my life. When I accepted the Lord in my life and was baptized, I went home and immediately tried to avoid doing anything that would remotely be considered sinful. I stopped listening to my favorite R&B records, believing that was the extent of sin in my life at the time (I didn't smoke, didn't drink, didn't party, and I wasn't sexually active). I had no interest in going to the hell that was so vividly described by my friend.

While no one reading this book would probably blame me for not wanting to go to a place filled with hellfire and brimstone, the problem is that my life became so focused on the devil and what he was doing that I had no clue about what God was doing. I came to this realization one day while looking at a news program—and watching one bad news report after another. Suddenly my soul began to cry out, "Is there any good news?" It was at that point that God gave me a revelation that my thoughts and my energies should be focused on the wondrous works of God wrought through his grace. I began to understand why so many Christians said that they no longer watched the news. I used to dispute this. Without watching the news, how would they have any idea what is going on in the world? How would they know what is going on in their own neighborhoods? But for them, not knowing what was going on was better than filling their minds and souls with a constant barrage of news of the devil's handiwork.

I began to switch my focus. Instead of paying attention to what Satan was doing, I needed to know what God was doing. And as I began to think about him—his goodness, his holiness, his grace, his mercy, his providence, his glory, his excellence, and his love—my soul and my spirit found joy and strength.

Romans 14:17 states, *"For the kingdom of God is not a matter of eating and drinking, but of **righteousness, peace and joy** in the **Holy Spirit**."* As I began to focus on God, the kingdom of God became realized within me. I was no longer a member of the earthly kingdom, with all of its pains, sorrows, and evils. Though in the flesh I am still a part of this world, my spirit and my soul are liberated from its bondage.

Romans 12:2 says, *"Do not conform any longer to the pattern of this world, but be transformed by the renewing of your mind. Then you will be able to test and approve what God's will is — his good, pleasing and perfect will."* Transformation takes place in our lives when our minds, our thoughts, our intellect, and our reason become subject to the word of God. When my thoughts became focused on him, it transformed me in such a way that I now have the ability to look at people and see the potential in them. I can see the good and positive things about people, despite their negative aspects. That ability has helped me in ministry. It is amazing to me how many people are willing to discard others based on a few character defects, while ignoring the tremendous potential that each child of God has within them. The more I dwell on God, the more my soul and my spirit become refreshed, and the Holy Spirit has the opportunity to perform the delicate surgery needed to liberate me from the sin and stain of this world.

Paul the apostle exhorts the Philippians with these words:

Finally, brothers, whatever is true, whatever is noble, whatever is right, whatever is pure, whatever is lovely, whatever is admirable — if anything is excellent or praiseworthy — think about such things (Philippians 4:8).

With the creative, intellectual mind of the introvert deeply focused on the true, noble, righteous, pure, lovely, admirable, excellent, and praiseworthy things of God, the potential exists for profound insights, unique perspectives, and anointed creative endeavors (music, books, drama, etc.) that can bless the Lord, encourage the saints, and transform the kingdom of God.

Quality #8: Introverts are less dependent upon others.

Typical introverts, because of their inner mental energy, their deep thinking, and their need for solitude, tend to develop skills and abilities that minimize their need for and reliance upon interpersonal contact. If we need to know something or need expertise in an area, we are more likely to pick up a book and read it or research the topic on the Internet rather than engage people who have those skill sets. This is not an antisocial act as much as it is a result of our need to stimulate ourselves intellectually and improve our ability for problem solving and analytical thought.

This does not mean that introverts do not need others. Kingdom Christians who desire to be spiritually healthy cannot isolate themselves from the need for and fellowship with other Christians. Despite the line of the song "Long as I got King Jesus, I don't need nobody else," all Christians need the fellowship, ministry, perspective, advice, and presence of other believers, and introverts are not exempt. Ephesians 4:11-16 speaks of our relationship to the body of Christ and our need for interconnectedness and unity in the body. But introverts, who tend to have a higher level of intelligence, are less likely to rely on others to solve problems for them.

This can also place many introverts at odds with God. Instead of praying to God for solutions to problems, introverts may try to figure out a solution which may or may not be in God's will and timing. On the other hand, it is equally bothersome to God to become slothful and to do nothing of one's own accord, using the promised blessings of God to become physically lazy and mentally idle. A few years ago, I heard one man say, "If God is going to bless me with finances, why do I need a job?" God expects us to use our skills and abilities to take care of ourselves.

There is support for this view in 1 Thessalonians 4:11-12:

Make it your ambition to lead a quiet life, to

mind your own business and to work with your hands, just as we told you, so that your daily life may win the respect of outsiders and so that you will not be dependent on anybody.

The last phrase above, *"so that you will not be dependent upon anybody,"* reads differently in the King James Version. In the King James Version, it states, *"and that ye may lack of nothing."* I shared both translations so that the reader will not walk away with the false impression that 1 Thessalonians 4:11-12 encourages us to be independent of the body of Christ for everything, and that we do not need the saints. On the contrary, we need one another. However, unless we are physically or mentally unable, we should not have to rely on others for *everything*, particularly our basic needs of food, water, shelter, and clothing.

It is indeed a blessing to be able to meet one's own needs. In 2005, I resigned from a high-paying position as a contractor to the United States Postal Service to work full time operating a post-prison transitional house for ex-prisoners. I made this decision because I realized that the transitional house was taking more of my time that I had anticipated, and I could not continue to maintain a full-time job and run the transitional house at the same time. Since the transitional house had the financial means to support me (though not at the level that I was being paid with the Postal Service), I resigned from the Postal Service and immediately began working full time for the transitional house.

Things rolled along well until 2008, when it became clear that the ministry was running out of money, and we could not continue to maintain the house or my salary. I supported myself for a while through savings, and then started a few online businesses through eBay and Amazon.com to generate income, but this was not enough to pay the bills. Occasionally I got support through offerings from my church. A dear sister in Christ blessed me greatly by giving me $200 a month in love offerings. Yet still, it was not enough to keep the bill collectors at bay.

My pastor, Bishop Paul Gaskins, suggested that I return to full-time employment. I resisted this suggestion at first, partially because of pride, and partially because I did not want to return to the daily grind of the "worldly" workforce. Though I tried to find employment initially, I never put great effort into it, because my hope was to be supported in ministry full time. However, my church is small, meager, and unable to support me in part-time ministry, much less full time. Meanwhile, my finances were steadily dwindling, and I became more and more dependent upon love offerings from the saints. It was clear that if my finances didn't improve, I would be evicted from my apartment, and my dependence upon the saints would take on a whole new dimension.

But that was where I drew the line. To be dependent upon the saints for a few bucks to pay the water bill is one thing, but to become homeless was another. I was determined not to let that happen.

In mid-2009 I threw myself into finding employment. I knew that God would bless me with a job once I stopped being prideful and put my *all* into it. I sent out several resumes and applications per day and checked out every job lead that came my way. I cast aside pride and opened myself up to jobs that I thought were beneath me. I was the chief of a non-profit organization, and here I was applying for jobs as a janitor (God knows exactly how to humble you). Only two months later, I was blessed to be hired as a manager of a nonprofit agency that I had previously partnered with in the ministry to ex-prisoners. It is a position that I hold to this day. God is good!

The pay for this position is nowhere near the pay I was receiving working at the Postal Service, and slightly less than what I was receiving through the transitional house. But fortunately, it was enough to pay the bills and break me out of needing to depend on the saints for money.

Though I love the members of my church, it is very liberating not to have to depend on them for my daily needs. Not only that, I am now in a position where I can give back to others who may be in need. As the old Billie Holiday song attests, "Mama may have, Papa may have, but God bless the child that's got his own."[14] I feel extremely blessed to be able to

---

14   "God Bless the Child," Billie Holiday and Arthur Herzog,

take care of my own needs.

I think this is the economic state that God encourages us to be in, a state where we do not have to depend on anyone for our own sustenance. I do not believe that God desires that we be in poverty[15], barely scraping up what we need to survive. Introverts, with their elevated IQ and intellectual prowess, have the capability to learn skills that will go a long way to helping them to take care of themselves. But even this has to be kept in perspective, so that we do not become more dependent upon our skills and abilities than we depend upon God (Mark 10:17-31).

Quality #9: Introverts are sensitive.

With the apparent "antisocial" reputation that in-

Jr., 1939.

15   The view that God does not desire us to be in poverty is often associated with so-called "prosperity theology." My view of this is that God has promised to take care of our needs (food, water, shelter, etc.), and that poverty is a fundamental inability to meet those needs. Prosperity theology is widely interpreted to mean that God wants us to obtain material wealth above and beyond that which is required to meet our basic needs. So, while I do not believe God wants us to be in poverty, it is a matter of one's individual relationship with God as to whether God has called them into accumulation of material wealth. Wealth accumulation is not necessarily what God calls of all Christians, and there are those who feel that God has called them to live simply, without lots of material trappings. However, in my estimation, living simply does not equate to poverty.

troverts have, they possess one quality that can endear them to many people. *Sensitivity* is the ability to respond compassionately, tactfully, and emotionally to the emotions or situations of others. Typical introverts possess such sensitivity and empathy, often to the point where that very same sensitivity may cause them emotional pain. Yes, it is easier to hurt the feelings of introverts, because, being so inner-directed, they are in tune with their own emotions and can empathize with the emotions of others.

However, it is their "thin skin" that can give introverts advantages in ministry and when dealing with others. Because of their sensitivity, they are less likely to dismiss outright the emotions of others, and are more likely to respond in an understanding, caring, and compassionate manner.

An introverted program manager at a small nonprofit housing counseling agency in Pennsylvania once related to me a story about an employee whom he had hired as a receptionist. She was responsible for making sure that the office was open each day, ensuring that telephone calls were answered promptly, and that visitors were received. For several months she did a great job, causing the program manager to believe that he had made a great decision in hiring her.

However, her performance began to wane after her initial months. She started to arrive at work late, if at all, and she would often snap at visitors and callers. The program manager met with her to try to determine what was going on, and he found out that the woman's husband had been arrested. She was now left to support three kids all by herself. One of the kids had started acting out in school, and that would cause her to be late or absent from work. The stress of raising the kids alone while trying to be supportive of her husband as he dealt with various phases of the criminal justice system made her irritable. It was difficult for her to put on a happy face at work when she was so miserable at home.

As she poured out her heart to the program manager, he couldn't help but feel for her. When she cried in his office while relating the stress and turmoil she was going through, it took every ounce of willpower for him to avoid crying himself. He knew about and identified with these emotions. As an introvert, he had been rejected, misunderstood, and turned down for promotions because he was not gregarious enough, and people thought of him as strange because he didn't talk much. Although he was married now, he had experienced many moments of loneliness in his life because he was not as romantically "forward" as his extroverted friends. At times, he felt just as abandoned, ostracized, and stressed out as the receptionist.

Now he understood why she was acting out at work. He identified with her. And although there was nothing he could do to help her out of her predicament, the least he could do was to be a little more tolerant at work. For as long as he could, he tried to work around her frequent absences and late arrivals.

But after a few weeks, it became almost unbearable. As the receptionist, she was the face of the organization to first-time visitors, and she needed to make a good impression on them. But most days, she was either too tired or too stressed to put on a nice face. When she was not at work, the program manager had to use one of the social workers to cover the front desk. This was an added burden to the social worker and affected her ability to serve her clients.

The program manager needed to make a decision. He knew he could not continue to distract his social workers and run the agency this way. At the program manager's request, the executive director, who worked at another site, tried to find her other openings within the agency where her frequent absences would have less of an impact. But there was nothing available, and the agency's tiny budget would not allow for a position to be created.

Seeing the handwriting on the wall, the program manager tried to enlist help from other nonprofits whose staff members could counsel the receptionist and help her better cope with the challenges she was facing. He was successful at getting her a referral to an agency that works with the children and families of prisoners (by this time, the receptionist's husband had been convicted and sentenced to three years in prison). She kept two or three appointments with the other agency, and then failed to follow up with subsequent appointments.

The program manager didn't know what else to do. Everywhere he turned, he hit a brick wall. His executive director was pressing him to take action because the receptionist did not follow through with all her appointments.

The program manager went into the executive director's office the next day and turned in his resignation letter, feeling as if he had no choice. When the executive director asked him why he was resigning, the program manager replied that he could no longer work for a company that would fire a woman in such dire straits. He knew that she would likely get fired anyway despite his resignation, but he would not be the one dropping the ax.

Throughout this experience, the program manager had heard fellow employees complain about the receptionist. They would say, *"Why doesn't she just fix her problems and come to work?"* They expected her to snap her fingers and solve her problems. But it is rarely that easy. The receptionist had a myriad of issues that made it difficult for her to be a faithful employee at work, and most of her issues would take a lot of time and effort to resolve.

For the program manager, his introversion allowed him to look deeper and get to the root of her problem, rather than assuming she was being lazy and irresponsible and using that as an excuse to fire her. His sensitivity allowed him to identify with her and respond appropriately and compassionately to her situation. And because his sensitivity would not allow him to fire a woman with challenging problems, instead he offered up himself rather than perform an act that would probably just make her situation worse, and violated every scruple and moral within him.

Fortunately, the executive director did not accept his resignation. Instead, he convened a meeting with his board of directors in which the receptionist was one of the main topics. In the exchange of ideas, the board members came up with several options that would allow the receptionist to remain employed while working out her issues. One option seemed to garner the most support from the group. Inspired by the passion and determination of the program manager, one of the board members decided to hire her at his law firm, giving her a backroom data entry position where her absences would have minimal impact on the firm. This way, she would remain employed and wouldn't join the homeless or welfare rolls.

Now the program manager had another problem. How would he present this to the receptionist without making her think that he was throwing her away and passing off a "problem child" to another organization? This concern was an aspect of his sensitive, introverted nature; he wanted to make sure that he minimized any ill feelings as a result of the transfer. He concluded that although she had no idea that he was willing to quit his job rather than fire her, he needed to tell her so that she understood that he was sensitive to her feelings and struggles.

After he was certain that everything was squared away with her employment at the law firm, the program manager talked to the receptionist about the transfer. To his delight, she was ecstatic about the transfer, as she had always wanted to work at a law firm. And she was honored that he was willing to put his job on the line for her.

The program manager and the receptionist remain friends to this day.

This is the impact that a sensitive introvert can have. The ability to connect with the emotions of others and respond in an appropriate, compassionate and caring manner is an absolute necessity for ministry. The Bible requires that same type of sensitivity in the body of Christ. Romans 12:15 says, *"Rejoice with those who rejoice; mourn with those who mourn."* In 1 Corinthians 12:26, it states, *"If one part suffers, every part suffers with it; if one part is honored, every part rejoices with it."* These scriptures acknowledge that there should be a level of sensitivity in the body of Christ such that we identify with and respond accordingly to the emotions of others. That can only happen to the extent that we are willing to be connected to one another, to delve deeper into one another through fellowship, and truly become brothers and sisters in Christ.

Another scripture which illustrates the sensitivity that we should have toward one another is in 1 John 3:17:

If anyone has material possessions and sees his brother in need but has no pity on him, how can the love of God be in him?

Being sensitive to one another is a direct result of love. It is something that is not just required of introverts, but of extroverts as well.

Finally, in 1 Peter 3:8:

Finally, all of you, live in harmony with one another; be sympathetic, love as brothers, be compassionate and humble.

Certainly, these aspects are required of all Christians, not just introverts. But introverts, with their inherent sensitivity, have an advantage in adhering to the scriptural mandate to be compassionate, sympathetic, and loving.

Quality #10: Introverts are mysterious.

And he said unto them, Unto you it is given to know the mystery of the kingdom of God: but unto them that are without, all these things are done in parables: (Mark 4:11, KJV).

The word *mysterious* tends to conjure negative connotations to those who are not familiar with the real meaning of the word. A person described as mysterious may be deemed to be eerie, or strange, or spooky, even dangerous; someone to be avoided at all costs. But the word *mystery* simply means something that is kept secret, unknown, or unexplained. As applied to introverts, it simply means that they prefer not to reveal much of themselves, or open up their lives, to people whom they do not know and do not trust. As mentioned previously, introverts often have a small but close circle of friends whom they trust implicitly, and it is within this group that introverts feel most comfortable sharing details about their lives, because it is only within this group of understanding individuals where they will derive any benefit from sharing their lives so openly.

This sense of mystery is also inherent in the kingdom of God. The Bible is one of the oldest, widely read, and influential books in the world, yet it is also one of the most mysterious. People have been trying to interpret its sayings since the very first words were written; yet for those who read the Word without the aid of the Holy Spirit, they are a mystery, or a secret, to them. God is not trying to make himself secretive for secrecy's sake; rather, because God exists in a spiritual realm, only those who also operate in that realm can fully comprehend the things of God. So, one must be born of the Spirit in order to fully understand and appreciate the Lord. As 1 Corinthians 2:14 says, *"The man without the Spirit does not accept the things that come from the Spirit of God, for they are foolishness to him, and he cannot understand them, because they are spiritually discerned."*

So, to those without the Spirit, God is a secret, a mystery, and an unknown. Trying to understand the mysteries of the kingdom is fruitless without walking in the realm of the Holy Spirit. Similarly, introverts live in another realm — one that is almost completely misunderstood by those outside it.

There are those who think that introverts are strange, weird, and even ungodly. But that is because they do not understand the realm that introverts live in. And, to borrow a phrase I once heard, "what people do not understand, they fear and reject."

Introverts may think that extroverts are loud, brassy, pushy, and ungodly. But again, it is because they do not understand extroverts. Throughout this book, I have tried not to pit introverts against extroverts, because I realize that each personality type has value and is needed in the kingdom of God. But because the numbers of them in this country pale in comparison to the number of extroverts, introverts are probably more maligned and misunderstood than extroverts.

In thinking about my introversion, I recognize this secretive quality within myself. If you were to look over my shoulder at what I am writing right now, I would likely try to keep you from seeing it. If you were to ask me what I am doing, I may tell you that I am writing a book, but I would not tell you what it is about. Some of my friends often call me *secret squir-*

rel, a term used in law enforcement and military circles, and derived from the old Hanna-Barbera cartoon. I had to do a lot of soul-searching to find out why I was this way. It is not because I am afraid of anything. I began to realize that I do not like to reveal anything until I am ready. My ideas must be well thought out and well prepared. I need to ensure that it will achieve the important and compelling purpose for which I am revealing it, and will not be detrimental to me or to others in any way. If revealing the information achieves no real purpose, I will just keep it to myself. This may create the unfortunate and inaccurate perception that introverts have something to hide or are being aloof. But it also can create a sense of intrigue about introverts and the things that they do.

Introverts are not only secretive with information about their own lives; they are also ideal people to present confidential information to, as they do not feel compelled to share that information with other people. Proverbs 11:13 states, *"A gossip betrays a confidence, but a trustworthy man keeps a **secret**."* Again, Proverbs 20:19 states, *"A gossip betrays a confidence; so avoid a man who talks too much."*

The ability to keep things in confidence is a biblically endorsed quality that fosters relationship and fellowship in the body of Christ. God is interested in developing trustworthy saints who will take great care with information that is shared with them. God abhors gossipers and slanderers (Romans 1:29-

32; 1 Timothy 5:12-13), and typical introverts are not known to be gossipers.

Even Jesus was secretive at times. In Mark 1:40-45:

> *A man with leprosy came to him and begged him on his knees, "If you are willing, you can make me clean." Filled with compassion, Jesus reached out his hand and touched the man. "I am willing," he said. "Be clean!" Immediately the leprosy left him and he was cured.*
>
> *Jesus sent him away at once with a strong warning: "See that you **don't tell this to anyone**. But go, show yourself to the priest and offer the sacrifices that Moses commanded for your cleansing, as a testimony to them." Instead he went out and began to talk freely, spreading the news. As a result, Jesus could no longer enter a town openly but stayed outside in lonely places. Yet the people still came to him from everywhere.*

Here, Jesus's reason for telling the man with leprosy not to tell anyone was because of the renown that would likely spread as a result. This renown would interrupt his ministry and his planned timeline, and make it difficult for him to prepare his apostles for ministry after his death, burial, and resurrection. When you're a person in demand like Jesus, sometimes it is best not to reveal to certain people what you are doing. Celebrities are known for entering towns or cities, taking care of their business, and then leaving without letting anyone, even the news media, know what they are doing. Such resulting attention would likely delay or hinder their purpose for coming.

Yet despite the many reasons for keeping things shrouded in mystery, there are instances where keeping secrets could be harmful. The natural inclination of the introvert to keep things secret should not be used to hide or conceal sinful behavior. As Isaiah 29:15 notes, *"Woe to those who go to great depths to hide their plans from the LORD, who do their work in darkness and think, 'Who sees us? Who will know?' "* Psalm 80:8 tells us, *"You have set our iniquities before you, our secret sins in the light of your presence."* It is clear that we may be able to hide our sins from man, but we cannot hide them from God. God sees all of our sins and iniquities. For that reason, the best approach is to confess our sins to God, and to any others who may have been affected by our sins (James 5:16). Satan loves to keep the sins of the saints cloaked in darkness. The best way to defeat Satan, and receive healing and forgiveness from God, is to put sin in the light of Jesus. In many cases, it also helps to confess your sin to a trusted pastor or minister so that you can receive help and accountability for those sins in your life.

For the introvert, who has a natural tendency to keep things private, this can be a great blessing to the body of Christ when it is applied with wisdom and

direction from the Holy Spirit. If not applied carefully, the introvert's private side can be used as an opportunity to conceal sins, which are best dealt with
by exposing them to the light of God.

Quality #11: Introverts are gentle (meek).

*Through patience a ruler can be persuaded, and a
gentle tongue can break a bone (Proverbs 25:15).*

It is interesting how extroverts are often considered to be strong and forceful, while introverts are
seen as weak and ineffectual. This may be because
of the gentle and humble nature of many introverts,
which is no doubt related to their sensitive nature.
But gentleness should in no way be confused with being weak. In fact, one of the strongest character traits
mentioned in the Bible is gentleness, and it is one of
the fruits of the Spirit in Galatians 5:22-23. Gentleness, as the scripture above reveals, can indeed break
a bone. This means that a gentle word or manner can
do more in difficult situations than threats or intimidation.

A person is gentle when they realize that someone is, or could be, fragile, and they act and speak
in ways that cause minimal harm. Like handling a
newborn baby, a gentle person deals with others so
as to cause the least amount of offense or trauma. Because they can be easily hurt or offended because of
their sensitive natures, introverts can identify with

the hurt feelings of others and conduct themselves in ways that minimize the pain that is caused.

When I was operating the transitional house for ex-prisoners, one of the residents got in a loud argument with the caretaker of the home over a curfew violation (all residents had to be in the house by 10:00 p.m., unless they were at their place of employment). The argument got so out of control that one of the other residents had to step in to prevent a fistfight. When I heard about it the next day, I summoned the resident who had committed the violation. Once he was in my office, I asked what had happened. He confessed to being late for the curfew, but felt he had a good reason for being late (he missed his bus and was unable to get back before curfew). As it was the policy of the house, the caretaker told the resident that he would still have to write up a rule violation report. At that point, the resident flew off the handle and started yelling in a loud voice, and the caretaker, not wanting to seem as if he was intimidated by the resident, followed suit and started yelling as well.

I knew I was dealing with someone with a short fuse. Situations such as this had to be handled gingerly, or they could result in an explosive outpouring of anger. I recognized that the resident was quite volatile, and knew I had to tread carefully.

I said to him in a gentle, nonconfrontational voice, "I know you feel as if you were not legitimately violating the rules, and I am not accusing you of lying to cover up the fact that you were late. I believe that you missed the bus, and I believe that is why you were late. But as true as that is, the fact is that you were still late. And the rule allows no exceptions unless you are working. If this sounds unfair, it is because you may have conditioned your mind to believe that if you have a valid excuse for breaking the rules, it is okay. This is the same mentality that led you to prison. Whatever you did that resulted in your prison sentence, you likely felt justified in doing it. Maybe you were trying to survive. Maybe you needed to protect yourself. Maybe you were supporting an addiction. Whatever it was, you felt you had a reason to do it, or you would not have done it. One of the keys in staying out of prison is to recognize that there are no excuses for wrongdoing. Even if you had what you feel is a good reason, it doesn't change the fact that it is wrong. And if I were to make an exception every time someone feels as if they have a good reason to break the rule, then everybody would be breaking it, and the rule becomes ineffective. So, the rules of this house are designed to challenge you to change your thinking. You have to realize that there is no excuse for doing wrong, even if you have a good reason. When you realize that, you are on the way to changing the mentality that will keep you in bondage for the rest of your life."

After my talk, the resident showed no hint of anger. He saw that the rule he had violated was designed to make him a better person, rather than a means to kick him out of the house or cramp his style. When presented this way, with my voice in a calm, nonconfrontational tone, he understood and appreciated what I had to say. But I had to handle him gently in order to avoid the fragile areas of his psyche that would likely tick him off again.

Even if he had been angry, my gentle tone and calm manner would have gone a long way in helping him calm down. As Proverbs 15:1 attests, *"A gentle answer turns away wrath, but a harsh word stirs up anger."*

James 3:17 makes clear that gentleness is a part of heavenly wisdom. *"But the wisdom that comes from heaven is first of all pure; then peace-loving, considerate, submissive, full of mercy and good fruit, impartial and sincere."*

And 2 Timothy 2:24-26 is a sage eye-opener to those who falsely believe feel that a forceful confrontation is the best way to solve problems:

> *And the Lord's servant must not quarrel; instead, he must be kind to everyone, able to teach, not resentful. Those who oppose him he must gently instruct, in the hope that God will grant them repentance leading them to a knowledge of the truth, and that they will come to their senses and escape from the trap of the devil, who has taken them captive to do his will.*

Finally, Colossians 3:12 speaks about our daily "fashion" choices:

Therefore, as God's chosen people, holy and dearly loved, clothe yourselves with compassion, kindness, humility, gentleness and patience.

The introvert may be seen as puny, weak, and a pushover because of his gentle spirit, but the introvert in Christ possesses one of the most powerful weapons to ward off Satan's attacks in our lives and in the lives of others. Gentleness is far from a defect in personality; it is a wonderful gift from the Holy Spirit to help us relate to one another and to foster fellowship and relationships in the body of Christ.

TV Character Analysis

One of the more interesting characters on TV was the police captain in the 1980s series *Hill Street Blues*. Frank Furillo, as portrayed by actor Daniel J. Travanti, demonstrated that it was possible to be in a high-profile leadership position, and to do it well, without being outspoken or socially outgoing. His character resembles that of an introvert for most of the series. He has a deep concern for the men under his command. He rarely raises his voice, even when angry. When giving advice to his men, it is brief and to the point. He exudes strength in his quietness, and few people dare to cross him. He feels somewhat uncomfortable with the politics of his office.

Aside from a passionate relationship with an assistant district attorney, a friendly — though contentious — relationship with his ex-wife, and a strong love for his son, he has no real close relationships outside the office (although he shares several close in-office relationships). Aside from the moral implications of his premarital sexual relationship with the assistant district attorney, he appears to have impeccable moral character.

For a study of a secure, confident. and strong introvert, you may want to obtain the DVDs of this series and watch this character in action.

Biblical Character Analysis

Barely twenty-five chapters in, the Bible presents what may be the first introvert. Jacob, the younger brother of Esau, came out of Rebekah's womb grabbing onto the heel of Esau. Previously, it had been prophesied to Rebekah that *"one people shall be stronger than the other; and the older shall serve the younger" (Genesis 25:23, NAS)*. Given current perceptions of introverts, it is easy to conclude that Jacob, the younger brother, would be stronger than Esau and is therefore the extrovert, and that Esau is the introvert. However, in verse 27, the scripture describes Esau as "a man of the field." This can be compared to the modern vernacular of "man about town," used to describe a man who is sociable and hangs out at all the hip and trendy places, and knows where all the hot spots are. Esau is the type of person many might want to befriend. He was cunning, action-oriented, physically strong, and a hunter.

By contrast, Jacob is described as *"a peaceful man, living in tents" (Genesis 25:27)*. Other translations describe him as a quiet man, or a mild man. These scriptures imply that Jacob enjoyed the quiet, indoor life more so than the active lifestyle of a hunter. Yet, according to prophecy, Esau was destined to serve his younger brother.

Jacob's quiet nature was obviously not a hindrance to the growth and development of the church. In fact, Jacob, the last of three patriarchs, who was later named Israel, had twelve sons, whose offspring would become the twelve tribes of Israel. Though Jacob was certainly not perfect and had his problems, God used this quiet man for great exploits in the kingdom of God.

Still Waters Run Deep

The Functioning of Introverts in the Kingdom

We have different gifts, according to the grace given us. If a man's gift is prophesying, let him use it in proportion to his[a] faith. If it is serving, let him serve; if it is teaching, let him teach; if it is encouraging, let him encourage; if it is contributing to the needs of others, let him give generously; if it is leadership, let him govern diligently; if it is showing mercy, let him do it cheerfully (Romans 12:6-8).

But eagerly desire the greater gifts. And now I will show you the most excellent way. If I speak in the tongues of men or of angels, but do not have love, I am only a resounding gong or a clanging cymbal (1 Corinthians 12:31 – 13:1).

Having shown that the introverted personality is in compliance with scripture, introverts can feel confident that they do not need to change or become more extroverted. God can use introverts just as they are, without the need to "come out of their shell."

Unfortunately, introverts often have to coexist in congregations that lean more toward the extroverted side.

According to a press release from Pyco, Inc., a psychological type marketing company, the United States is 52 percent extroverted.[16] Some studies indicate that the United States is 75 percent extroverted. Whatever the number, it is clear that there are more extroverted people in the United States than extroverted ones.

Generally, churches in America are a reflection of their immediate communities, and the church in general is a reflection of the country. It can reasonable to assume that if the country is majority extroverted, so is the church. The talents and abilities of extroverts are often needed to plant and draw people to churches. As a result, extroverts head most churches, and their practices are often geared to extroverts.

However, there are several practices of the modern-day church that may be highly uncomfortable for many introverts. I have listed some of those practices below.

---

16   "PYCO Reveals America's Top 10 Most Extroverted Cities," accessed 7/22/12 from pycoscores.com.

The passing of the peace

The passing of the peace is a beloved practice in many churches. It is observed in a variety of ways, depending on the church tradition. It typically occurs during or after the service and involves approaching several people in the congregation, shaking hands or hugging, and saying "the peace of the Lord be with you." The person greeted will typically respond, "And also with you." Variations of the greeting may be used, or it may be discarded altogether in favor of whatever greeting is preferred by the individuals doing the greeting. It is usually brief, no more than two to fifteen minutes, depending on local tradition and the size of the congregation. It is a practical expression of the scripture in John 14:27, which states, *"Peace I leave with you; my peace I give you. I do not give to you as the world gives. Do not let your hearts be troubled and do not be afraid."*

The passing of the peace is practiced in my own church, and I rather enjoy it. Since it does not last too long in my church (usually two or three minutes), it is not as draining for me as other, lengthier social practices. It usually does not require long conversation, and there aren't a particular number of people you are required to greet. The celebration helps to unify the body of Christ, and helps to preserve the bond of peace among members (Ephesians 4:3). However, there are some aspects of the practice that can be challenging for introverts.

In some churches, passing of the peace often involves hugging strangers. Hugging strangers is unsettling for some people, whether they are introverts or extroverts. For many introverts, hugging is an intimate act, and they are not likely to feel comfortable engaging in it with people they barely know. Although I attend a hug-friendly church, greeting a stranger with a hug is normally not my first inclination. Saying hello, or maybe a handshake, is quite enough for me. Of course, some may believe that this is not because of my introversion, but because I am a man. And in their defense, a 2009 survey suggested that men actually preferred less hugging and other "intimate" activities in church.[17] But even as a child, I do not recall much hugging, kissing, or other acts of affection. It doesn't mean that I wasn't loved, or that I didn't love. It just means that I chose not to show my affection in this way.

Passing of the peace that involves greeting many people or lasts long may also be troublesome for introverts. Because of introverts' limited social energy, we are likely to get drained after a few greetings and, at the risk of seeming antisocial or aloof, refuse to shake any more hands or greet any more people. However, it may be tolerable if the introvert knows the people whom he is greeting.

My experience with passing of the peace may not be typical. I worship with a congregation of fewer

17   "Men want more anthems and less hugging in church," ChristianityToday.com, May 6, 2009.

than one hundred people, and some of the people in my congregation I have known for many years. So, my comfort level with passing of the peace in my church is higher than, say, the introvert who is visiting my church for the first time. But generally, introverts may have issues with the level of interaction involved with the passing of the peace, particularly if it is long, or if it involves relatively intimate practices such as hugging or kissing.

But if introverts have problems with a part of worship that is rooted in scripture, isn't that an indictment of introverts? Not necessarily. The passing of the peace is an inherent and life-giving part of many worship services. However, I should note that *nowhere in the Bible is there a scripture that mandates approaching several people in a worship service and greeting them.* In some churches, the practice of passing of the peace has become meaningless and hollow because it is done out of obligation and because it is an expected part of the service. It is just a ritual, devoid of any real, lasting benefit or any real, genuine feeling. If the real intent is to "pass the peace," what if there is someone in the congregation who is not at peace? Are the words themselves going to help? Maybe, but maybe not. And if not, is there a provision to delve deeper to find out why the person is not at peace and find out what can be done to help? If the practice is just ritual, that's another reason why introverts are loath to participate. But if there is real, true concern for the peace of people rather than just the empty recitation of words, introverts will often be the first to transcend surface-level empty talk, delve deeper, and try to find out why the person is not at peace. In that way, introverts can work more intimately with preserving the bond of peace than a ritual during a worship service.

The acknowledgment of visitors

In an effort to make their first-time visitors feel special and welcome, many churches acknowledge visitors during the worship service. This is done in varied ways, depending on the church, but it involves, at a minimum, reading the names of the visitors, along with asking them to stand to be recognized. Some churches go further by asking them to say something, or having them wear visitor name tags, or by bringing them to the front of the congregation so that others can welcome them with handshakes or hugs. While this may be a blessing to the extroverted visitor, this practice is likely to make introverts cringe.

We acknowledge visitors at our church by having them stand wherever they are and introduce themselves. No instruction is given other than that, so they are free to say as much, or as little, as they please. Most simply say their names and who invited them, while others embark on a full- fledged sermon that sometimes has to be cut short by the pastor. I have looked in the faces of those who are asked to stand and introduce themselves, and I have seen a few that are clearly uncomfortable with the practice. They may be shy, introverted, or both. When I have visited small churches, I am often asked to stand and say a few words. This is difficult, because at the time I may not have much to say, unless I had anticipated it beforehand and prepared some brief comments. But I am hardly the type that can come up with profound and interesting words at a moment's notice. If I can just say my name and who invited me, that would be fine. But if I have to do more than that, I will have issues.

This practice, which is typically observed in smaller, more social churches, puts the introvert, if only for a few seconds, at the center of attention. All eyes are on him or her. For a moment, no one is thinking about God or Jesus. No one is meditating. No one is paying attention to the pulpit. All focus is on that visitor, and that is nerve-racking for introverts. It drains the person of energy to have so much focus on him or her. A few people would not be so bad, but an entire congregation is brutal. Again, it has nothing to do with fear, but simply the way that introverts are designed.

Churches that wish to be welcoming to their newcomers (and that is a good thing) often design their welcoming strategy for the extrovert on both the welcoming and receiving end. While some people wouldn't mind being openly welcomed (during a passing of the peace, for instance), and be offended if they weren't, some people on the more introverted scale have no problem enjoying the service, and then slipping out without being formally welcomed. Different people prefer different modes of welcoming.

I know at least one church that encourages visitors who wish to be welcomed after service to stand in an area of the church designated for that purpose. That way, whoever wants to be welcomed by many adoring handshakes and hugs will likely feel appreciated, while others could simply slip out the door. Or maybe one person could be assigned to greet all visitors, either when they arrive or when they leave.

Public prayer petitions

Like everyone else, introverts need prayer. And they have no problem with making their prayer requests known to a few trusted people. But in some nonliturgical churches, there is a prayer time, either after the sermon or after the service is over, where the person who needs prayer comes to the pulpit and receives prayer from one or more ministers. Another related practice is when the minister talks about a particular subject and asks people to raise their hands if they need prayer in that area. Then, they are either prayed for where they stand or sit, or they are asked to come to the pulpit to receive prayer. The benefit of this practice is that it gives people the opportunity to be prayed for immediately, rather than waiting until the service is over, when they may be distracted and forget to seek prayer. Prayer can be administered immediately, while the Spirit is still moving. Again, introverts are likely to have challenges with this practice, as it forces them to risk others knowing about their prayer requests, and it places them at the center of attention.

I have often heard ministers, once their sermons are completed, calling for people to come up to the front and be prayed for. Often, the prayer petition is directly related to the sermon just preached. If no one responds, the minister may change his prayer petition, trying to get someone to admit his need for prayer and answer his petition by either raising his hand or approaching the pulpit. But what is interesting is that even though the minister made a prayer call from the pulpit, some people will wait until the service is over and ask privately for prayer. It does not take a rocket scientist to know that many people, especially introverts, are private people and do not want their prayer requests known by the general population, or may not want anyone to know that they need prayer. Many simply do not want to be the topic of "gossiping" churchgoers.

One of the faster-growing crimes today is identity theft, where a person will use their knowledge of your personal information, such as your social security number, your bank account number, your address, or your credit card information, and use it for their own personal benefit. But long before the term *identity theft* became a part of our national lexicon, gossips have been using other people's personal information for their own benefit. How? Because *gossips* thrive on getting information that no one else knows, or that is private and sharing it with others. They get great pleasure for being the renowned "information source" for many in their circles.

Unfortunately, the information they get is often secondhand, or devoid of proper explanation and perspective. When shared, it will make the person to whom the information pertains subject to false rumors, vicious innuendo, and other negative effects. This can damage a person's reputation and credibility, and could have far-reaching effects, such as damaging a person's ministry, or cause the person to lose a job.

I know of one instance where a gossip caused damage to a person's reputation. Claire was employed as an IT support technician for a large company. Her coworker, Rachel, had recently moved to share an office with her and sat in the cubicle directly across from her. One day, Claire got a support call from a male colleague, Mitchell, on another floor. Mitchell was much more adept at technology than Claire, and she picked his brain quite a bit. Rachel left her cubicle to go in the hallway to get a soda, and managed to overhear Claire say Mitchell's name on the phone just before she walked out the door.

When Rachel returned two minutes later and sat

down at her cubicle, she could hear Claire talking on the phone in hushed tones. The cubicle walls were so thin that she could hear everything that Claire was saying, despite the whispering. It sounded like Claire was making a date for an intimate dinner, and even told the caller that she loved him.

Rachel put two and two together and concluded that the married Claire was making a hot date with single guy Mitchell.

Armed with gossip fodder, she went around to all of her office friends, spreading the news like fertilizer on a plant bed. Interestingly enough, although most of the employees on that floor knew about the "hot date" that Claire had with Mitchell, none of that information made its way to either Claire or Mitchell. Of course, over the next few days, every time they saw Claire with Mitchell, it only fueled the rumors even more.

Bernard heard the rumors. Bernard was friends with Claire's husband and had been instrumental in getting Claire the job at the company. The moment he heard the rumors, he dialed Claire's husband and told him what he had heard. Of course, Bernard was not able to give Claire's husband specific dates, times, or even who said what—a common problem with gossip that has been passed through many "hands." For Claire's husband, however, the news was easy to believe. It confirmed why Claire had become so distant and standoffish lately.

Claire's husband waited until Claire came home

that evening and confronted her with the rumors. She denied the rumors and concluded that someone was lying and trying to set her up. She had no idea that it was Rachel who had started the rumors, and that the rumors had started when Rachel overheard her talking on the phone with Mitchell.

Claire's husband wanted to believe her, but found it difficult. Though he accepted her explanation and did not argue about it further, the incident introduced a spirit of distrust into their relationship that was very difficult to recover from. Although no infidelity had occurred between Claire and Mitchell, she and her husband eventually separated and divorced.

A marriage was dissolved because of a gossip-driven rumor, fueled by a false assumption by Rachel that the person whom Claire was talking to when Rachel left the office (Mitchell) was the same person who Claire was talking to when Rachel returned (her actual husband). Although Claire's marriage had its difficulties before the incident, an unsubstantiated rumor from an office mate sealed the fate of the marriage.

For this reason and others, many people want to keep their private information private. They want the ability to control and monitor any information about them that sees the light of day. To introverts, this is not an option. It is a necessity. For this reason, they will not be open to public prayer petitions, but will readily request private prayers from those whom they know will handle their information in the strictest confidence.

Forced social encounters

Churches that have made the Christian faith integral with the heightened social aspect of fellowship may make a mistake that will turn off many introverts. Similar to the custom of arranging marriages that is practiced in some cultures around the world, some churches have a practice of arranging relationships, usually in the form of assigning people in the congregation to build relationships with one or more disciples or mentors.

Often, the arrangements do not take into consideration the temperament of the parties involved. If a person who is introverted is assigned to an extroverted person, and neither of the parties understands the other's temperament, the relationship can be frustrating and unfruitful for all involved. Extroverted people, who typically have no problem picking up the phone, may not understand why their introverted friend doesn't call much. And an introverted person may think an extroverted friend is loud and brash, and may get worn out quickly being around them.

These types of arrangements often do not take into consideration the way in which many introverts develop relationships. For the extrovert, he may meet someone at the bus stop and wind up talking with him for several hours. As an introvert, relationships rarely happen for me that way. My friendships are more likely to develop over a period of time, usually after some level of interaction and observation has taken place. For many of my friendships, I strain to remember exactly when we became friends or the circumstances behind it, because the friendship was a natural progression from some degree of exposure to the individual over time.

I remember a good friend who I treasured and enjoyed spending time with. I first encountered her when I was working as a data entry clerk at a downtown D.C. firm. Silvia worked in an office down the hallway from mine, and I had no interaction with her other than the occasional "hello" as I passed by her office on the way to mine. Even during those rudimentary greetings, I found her to be somewhat standoffish and unfriendly.

Those occasional "hellos" were the extent of our encounters, until the firm moved from downtown D.C. into an office building in nearby Maryland. As a result of the move, she was assigned a cubicle directly next to mine. At the same time, my responsibilities evolved from a mere data entry clerk into a part-time IT support specialist, which gave me the opportunity to get out of my office and interact with many of the other employees at the firm. Even though Silvia was right next door, I had very little opportunity to directly interact with her until I became an IT person and had to help her fix technical issues with her computer. My entry in her work life as an IT tech led directly into an entry into her personal life, as she eventually asked me to help her and her husband fix some technical issues at home. I agreed.

The invitation to her and her husband's home was a beginning of a friendship that blossomed as we found we had much in common with each other, including playing chess and tinkering with computers. I once found Silvia unapproachable and aloof. In reality, she was one of the warmest, friendliest people I have met.

In retrospect, I realize she was an introvert like me.

The relationship did not happen as a result of customary social introductions. Neither one of us "broke the ice"; the ice just sort of gradually melted. The relationship was not forced; it gradually evolved as both of us moved beyond our period of observation and discovered things in common that resulted in a great friendship. When I look back over my life, I realize that most of my friendships have developed in this way.

Forced relationships are difficult for many introverts because it violates their natural need to observe and interact before acting. It obliterates the opportunity for trust to build naturally. It does not allow the introvert to appropriately vet the person to determine whether this is someone whom they want to allow into their inner circle. It gives no room to allow the Holy Spirit to draw people to one another.

And while the need for discipleship and mentoring is highly important (Deuteronomy 6:4-7; Matthew 22:37-40), these relationships can best be developed by observing who would be natural and spiritually redemptive matches rather than forcing people together who may be like oil and water.

Proverbs 12:26 affirms the need for Christians, whether introverted or extroverted, to be careful with whom they allow into their inner circles:

A righteous man is cautious in friendship, but the way of the wicked leads them astray.

I am confident that as God, through the Holy Spirit, works within introverts, he will draw them to people whom he desires them to interact with. God will also draw people to them, and perhaps they can be a positive influence in each other's lives. By allowing the Holy Spirit to move, the Lord can develop relationships just like the one between Paul and Priscilla and Aquila (Acts 18:2-3; 18-19, 26; Romans 16:3-4; 1 Corinthians 16:19; and 2 Timothy 4:19). The church that allows this to happen, rather than forcing it in the name of discipleship, fosters a social environment where people feel connected, affirmed, and valued.

What About this So-Called Comfort Zone?

"Love the LORD *your God with all your heart and with all your soul and with all your strength"* *(Deuteronomy 6:5).*

A few years ago, a fellow minister asked me to participate in an evangelism ministry. The ministry involved going door-to-door, issuing tracts and talking to people about the gospel. After some consideration, and determining whether this was something that God wanted me to do, I declined the invitation. When the minister asked me why, I explained that I did not think I was a good fit for the ministry. The minister rejected this reasoning and explained that if I was to be effective in heeding God's call, I needed to step outside of my comfort zone.

Much has been preached and taught about the "comfort zone" in Christianity. The phrase "coming out of the comfort zone" has become a popular catchphrase for ministers and preachers to describe the need for Christians to step out in faith and do things for God that may cause them fear or anxiety. Many people who are called by God to accomplish a task, to change an aspect of themselves, or to move forward in ministry often failed to do so because of their fear of losing something valuable. The loss could be, among others, money, friends, time, a career, independence, or even a sense of security. The lesson of the rich young ruler in Mark 10:17-22 is that, because of his dependence upon and fear of losing his many possessions, he squandered the opportunity to gain eternal life and submit his life to the authority of Jesus Christ.

The term "comfort zone" is a psychological term that has been appropriated by the church for use in ministry. Alasdair A.K. White, in his work, *From Comfort Zone to Performance Management*, describes it this way:

> 'The comfort zone is a behavioural state within which a person operates in an anxiety-neutral condition, using a limited set of behaviours to deliver a steady level of performance, usually without a sense of risk.'[18]

18   White, Alasdair A.K. *From Comfort Zone to Performance*

In simplified psychological parlance, the comfort zone is a state of being that feels safe, devoid of fear and risk.

Each one of us, regardless of temperament, have comfort zones, areas in our lives where we settle in, comfy and cozy, and avoid risk. We have those zones in our personal, professional, and church lives. These are areas where we feel most settled because risk is not a part of the equation.

From a kingdom perspective, risk is a natural part of living life in Christ. Faith itself involves risk. Faith is the substance of things hoped for, the evidence of things not seen (Hebrews 11:1). It involves trusting in things that, from our natural frame of reference, have not yet been shaped into reality. It involves trusting in the person of Jesus Christ who, from our fleshly perspective, is virtually invisible. A person who desires to flow into kingdom dynamics can no longer operate in a spiritual comfort zone.

One may be tempted, however, to assume that the introverted personality is part of a comfort zone; that in order to be effective in the kingdom of God, one must step out of introversion and into the more socially acceptable norms of extroversion.

Truth be told, as an introvert, I have had to function in my more extroverted self in order to accomplish some things that I felt that God was calling me

---

Management: Understanding Development and Performance, 2008, 3.

to do. There were times when I *had* to go to that meeting instead of just staying home and reading a book. There were moments I *had* to give a testimony before the congregation when my inclination was to remain silent. In these instances and others, I found it necessary to tap into that smaller portion of extroversion that is in most introverts. For extroverts, the opposite is also true.

However, functioning as an introvert cannot be defined in terms of a comfort zone.

For starters, stepping out of a comfort one involves taking risks. For the shy person to come out of his or her comfort zone involves risking rejection and the heightened sense of anxiety resulting from it. But for the non-shy introvert, there is no anxiety involved in tapping into our extroverted selves. Introversion is the way we were created to function, and fear and anxiety are not the basis of it. For this reason, the concept of a comfort zone is not applicable to introverts. Introversion does not represent a comfort zone any more than being black, white, male, or female represents a comfort zone. I am a male, and I am comfortable with being a male. Does it mean that I have to step outside of my maleness in order to do the will of God? A comfort zone is performance based. God does not call us to a wholesale change in personality and temperament just to perform adequately for him. God can use both introverts and extroverts just as they are.

How Introverts Can Function Successfully in the Church

So how does God use introverts? Given their natural temperament, how can introverts fit in the church, especially in the midst of extroverted churches? Should introverts leave their churches and seek out congregations that are more introverted?

I'll answer the last question first. The introvert must rely on the leading of the Holy Spirit as to what church to attend. God calls introverts to largely extroverted churches because their unique strengths can be beneficial to the church at large, and God needs both temperaments in a healthy, functioning church. In order to function successfully, however, the pastor must recognize the introvert's unique personality and be willing to structure programs and ministries such that all people, introverts and extroverts, can participate, feel welcomed and valued.

So how can introverts function successfully and effectively in the church with a minimal amount of frustration? What things can introverts participate in that are compatible with his or her natural, introverted tendencies? Some practical suggestions for introverts are below.

Educate your church leaders about temperament.

Unless your church leadership is familiar with psychology, has had some exposure to the Myers-Briggs Type Indicator®, or has done studies into human temperament, your leadership may not understand introverts to the extent that they can minister effectively to them. Many extroverted leaders simply assume introverts are shy or antisocial and may try to change them into extroverts, often without realizing what they are doing. Extroverted leaders may outright reject introversion, concluding that it is God's will to be outgoing and extroverted.

People who understand introversion or who are introverts are the best ones to try to inform their extroverted leaders about introverts, using many of the truths found in this book and other books about the subject. The goal is to get the leadership to realize the need to accommodate both types of people, and to work with them to structure the church and its ministries and programs to be receptive to both introverts and extroverts.

What if the church leadership is not receptive to engaging introverts? A situation such as this requires much thought and much prayer. It is important to remain in tune with the leading of Holy Spirit, and you may need to decide whether the Holy Spirit has truly led you to the congregation you are now attending. But I should caution you on one thing: just because your church leadership does not embrace introversion is not necessarily a reason to pack up and leave your church. It may be that God is calling you there to pray and continue to work with the church leadership until such a time as their hearts and minds are changed, and that may happen through your influence and your passion. Many reforms in churches have occurred because one person stayed and effected change. This person didn't run away because things didn't immediately suit his or her taste. Remember, running away usually doesn't work; it is highly unlikely that anyone will ever find the perfect church.

Join or start a small group.

And let us consider one another to provoke unto love and to good works: Not forsaking the assembling of ourselves together, as the manner of some is; but exhorting one another: and so much the more, as ye see the day approaching (He-

brews 10:24-25, KJV).

Despite introverts' natural tendency to limit their time with people, they nonetheless need opportunities to fellowship, to share their hearts, to minister, and to receive strength, knowledge, and encouragement from others. The word "fellowship" is derived from the ancient Greek word *koinonia*, which means, "communion by intimate participation."[19] We spoke of the word *intercourse* earlier as associated with fellowship. As Hebrews 10:24-25 states, no person should live in a cocoon, but should seek opportunities for close relationship and sharing with one another.

For introverts, this is best done in a small-group environment, consisting of no more than ten to twelve people. This provides the introvert with a consistent group of people with whom he or she can build relationships, while limiting the amount of people that the introvert has to deal with—thus minimizing the energy drain.

In addition, small groups are one of the best ways for the church to cater to and minister to persons of various temperaments. Groups can be designed for persons who are introverts, and the activities of that group can be tailored to the unique needs of the group. A group such as this may place less emphasis on impromptu conversation and more on worship,

19   Wikipedia contributors, "Koinonia," Wikipedia, The Free Encyclopedia, http://en.wikipedia.org/w/index.php?title=Koinonia&oldid=471631142 (accessed December 1, 2012).

prayer, meditation, and other activities that engage the inner person and his or her connection to God. Over time, vital relationships are built between and among members of the group, and more in-depth and intimate discussion and conversation can take place.

The gathering places of these groups are important as well. Rather than gathering in a large church hall or an institutional environment, meetings can take place at members' homes, or in smaller, private rooms of the church. This creates more of a personal, intimate environment, presents less of an opportunity for others outside the group to eavesdrop and observe what is going on, and is well suited to introverts who like to keep things private and do not want everyone in the church knowing their business.

While small groups are a good way for introverts to connect with others, it is not in any way a panacea. Some introverts may feel intimidated by the small group because of the added pressure to share their lives and to talk with others, particularly if the group consists of people they do not know initially. In this instance, it is best for a small group to come to fruition organically rather than be forced. Most friendships occur organically, rather than either party being told, pressured, or even influenced into friendships with the other person. The introvert can also gather the people in the congregation that he already knows and trusts, and who know one another, and bring them together as a group to meet either informally or formally for worship, prayer, and fellowship.

Participate in creative arts ministries.

The world of creative arts, such as drama and the performing arts, graphic and visual arts, writing, film, and music is a natural fit for introverts, primarily because these endeavors have some elements that the introvert can do alone. Many a great play, painting, novel, song, or statue was created in an empty room by an introvert with many moments of uninterrupted solitude. I have at various times in my life excelled at all of these endeavors, and I currently engage in all but one (music).

You may be tempted to dispute the performing arts and music performance as a good fit for introverts. After all, these things are often done in front of crowds. And aren't crowds intimidating for introverts?

There's another fear word: *intimidation*. Crowds do not intimidate non-shy introverts. They just easily drain us, particularly if there is a high level of personal interaction. Performing arts and musical events are often prepared beforehand, thought out, and rehearsed. During the performance, there is little personal interaction (although one may choose to add personal interaction, such as answering questions from the audience, praying for people during or after the show, or mingling with the crowd after the performance).

Introverts may consider participating in one or more of the following areas according to talent (this is not an exhaustive list):

- The music ministry, including the choir, praise and worship teams, instrumentalist, soloist, music instructor, composer, etc.
- The drama ministry, including playwriting, acting, stage management, lighting and sound, set design, etc.
- The church decorating committee.
- The film and video ministry.
- The church newsletter.
- Sound technician.
- Audiovisual recording.
- Lighting technician.
- Dance ministry.
- Sermon visual media.
- Photography.

All of these options provide the introvert with an opportunity to minister and participate in the life of the church without extensive personal interaction that could be draining.

Social networking or online participation.

Social networking sites such as Facebook and Twitter, Christian sites such as Shoutlife and God-Tube, and Christian blog sites allow introverts to build relationships and interact with others on their own terms. Because these and other social networking sites remove the pressure to respond immediately, they allow introverts to respond with more thought-out, creative, and engaging comments as opposed to being put on the spot and responding awkwardly, or even inappropriately. Churches that embrace introverts may want to allow them to participate in the social networking and web strategy of the church, since they are typically much more comfortable communicating online rather than in person.

A few months ago, one of the members of my church, who saw me as a potential father figure, indicated that he wanted to connect with me on a personal level. He knew my tendency to communicate primarily via e-mail and text. He wanted to connect with me on *his* terms. He rejected outright my use of e-mail and text, saying it was impersonal and not the way to communicate in the body of Christ. Of course, this person is highly extroverted and sparingly uses e-mail and text.

I responded out of my extroverted side and connected with him on his terms as the Lord led me. And there are times, such as when a person has an immediate, urgent need to speak with me, that e-mail and text are certainly not appropriate. But I tell people that if they communicate with me via e-mail, text, or social media, their answer may not be immediate, but they are more likely to get a complete, well-thought-out, and engaging answer from me versus talking to me on the phone or in person. For this reason, social media and having an online presence is a haven for introverts who can share ideas, information, and insight without pressing immediacy.

Introverts who attend churches without a web or social networking presence may consider working with their church leadership to establish such a presence.

Mentoring and Discipleship.

> *Therefore go and make disciples of all nations, baptizing them in the name of the Father and of the Son and of the Holy Spirit, and teaching them to obey everything I have commanded you. And surely I am with you always, to the very end of the age (Matthew 28:19-20).*

At first glance, this may not appear to be the ideal pick for an introvert. This is only because of the common misconceptions that introverts do not like people and hate to deal with them.

On the contrary, introverts do not dislike people. Many of them like people. You will often find that introverts are some of the most loving, caring, compassionate, and sensitive people around. Most people do not know this, because introverts do not openly advertise these qualities. Yet people who have taken the time to get to know introverts report that they are some of the best friends they have met.

These qualities bode well in a mentoring ministry, especially one that is geared toward discipleship. But, just as with small groups, a mentoring relationship must be built organically. In other words, the best way for an introvert to build a mentoring relationship is by caring for a person and being ready for openings to minister and share Christ.

Matthew 28:19 calls for every Christian to make disciples of all nations. But the scripture does not describe the methods and processes to follow to engage people and bring them to Christ, or encourage them in their already-existing walk with Christ. This is because those methods will be different depending upon the individual and his or her unique gifts and temperament. There is no *one size fits all* when it comes to discipleship. Unfortunately, most of the methods of discipleship taught in today's churches involve an extroverted approach tailored to people who are quick on their feet and can give quick answers to almost every question. They also do not take into consideration those people who may not respond so well to an extroverted approach.

If most introverts are like me, they cannot stand it when someone tries to hard-sell them something, even if that something is the gospel. They will immediately turn off with such an approach, because introverts like to think about things before they make decisions. Conversely, introverts, when presenting the gospel, rarely do it in a pushy manner, but are most likely to share the gospel through their lifestyles and their loving actions more so than words. They will use words when necessary, but won't do it to the extent that extroverts do.

I am grateful today for the people who have come into my life. They shared their lives and extended Christian love to me, yet infrequently spoke about Christ or the gospel directly. I knew they were Christian because of the love they had for me, and because of their worship and praise. These people have contributed to my perception of Christ, and have watered me as I grew in the grace and knowledge of Christ. These people never said to me, "don't do this" or "don't do that," but I learned about the proper way to live through their lifestyles. These are people who never invited me to go to church, yet I wanted to go simply to be around them. Today as I write this, I mourn the evident loss of the ability to "show we are Christians by our love for one another" in many of today's churches. We have become more about programs, entertainment, and capitalistic pursuits than truly loving one another.

I can't tell you how many people have told me they knew there was "something about me" before they found out I was a minister. That "something" is the love of the Lord, the anointing of the Holy Spirit. This creates opportunities for me to minister the gospel. Even if people are drawn to you, they may not be perceptive or intuitive enough to know how to get to the place where you are. This is where preaching and teaching come in.

The church in America is an extroverted, talking church. We say a lot. But do we live out the substance of what we are saying? Or is our talk full of empty words without testimony or example? It is in that area that I believe introverts who are living according to the Word can be invaluable in the discipleship strategy of any church.

Preaching and teaching.

Who says that verbal proclamation of the word of God is strictly an extroverted exercise? Some of the greatest teachers and preachers in America are introverts. I'd tell you who they are, but you likely would not know any of them. And they likely prefer it that way. These unsung preachers do not draw huge crowds or fill stadiums. They do not have bestselling books on the shelves at Walmart. But they have done as much to elevate the body of Christ and bring people into the kingdom as any preacher you will see on television or on the Internet.

Introverted preachers are best when they have had an opportunity to prepare their remarks before the sermon. They are not off-the-cuff preachers who can come up with a formal sermon on a moment's notice.

A John Wesley quote is popular among some preachers. It says, "Always be ready to preach, ready to pray, and ready to die." Other variations add the words "within five minutes." As popular as the saying is, it is obviously geared toward extroverts, and I know that many introverts, including me, would have struggles with formalized preaching on such short notice.

But what if someone approached me and asked me to preach the gospel to them, and preach it now? What if this person needed and wanted salvation? It is to these informal situations that I think John Wesley's quote is most applicable. Even as an introvert, I need to be ready to give hope at a moment's notice. But to give a forty-five-minute sermon? I need some prep time.

Because of introverts' penchant for deep thinking, they are poised to bring messages and teach lessons that are lifesaving and life-affirming. It may take them a few days to pull the sermon together, but once it is done, it can be quite profound. I used to decry that it took me two to three days to come up with a good sermon. I thought I should be able to come up with one in about two to three hours. Understanding my temperament, I now accept that it may take me a while to write a good sermon, but it will be well thought out and have an impact once it is done.

Introverts who are called to preach and teach need to be allowed time to prepare their remarks and not

be expected to come up with something immediately.

> *Men of genius are not quick judges of*
> *character. Deep thinking and high*
> *imagining blunt that trivial instinct by*
> *which you and I size people up.*

Max Beerbohm

Become accountable.

If you are in a church with extroverted leaders,
this is an important aspect of successful functioning
in the church. Your extroverted leaders want to get
to know you. And you will not do them, or yourself, any favors by denying them that opportunity.
But unless you have succeeded in educating your
church leaders about temperament, your leaders
may grow increasingly suspicious of you, and may
wonder what it is you have to hide. For many extroverts, they tend to feel more comfortable with a person when he or she is talking, outgoing, and expres-
sive. Even though they may not agree with what the
person is saying, at least they know their thoughts
and have some idea of what to expect from them.
They may not be as clear, however, when it comes to
introverts.

The panacea is for your church leaders to under-

stand introverts and to give you room to build relationships on your own terms. If that is not the case in
your church, then you will need to pray for God to reveal to you the one person in your leadership whom
you can feel comfortable with sharing the most intimate details of your life. You should give this person
entrance to minister to you, lead you in discipleship,
and provide you guidance and care. In evangelical
parlance, this person is called your "spiritual covering." Just as you can provide discipleship and mentoring to others, this person can provide discipleship
and mentoring to you.

There are two reasons why this is important. First
of all, the principle of spiritual covering is presented
all through the Bible as a means to provide care and
blessings to the saints and help them mature through
a practical, one-on-one relationship. Naysayers may
say that spiritual covering is a means of spiritual control, but this is not what the Bible intends.

Second, when you are under spiritual covering
and have established such a relationship with a leader in your church, you are less likely to be subject to
suspicion and more likely to be trusted. Most leaders,
myself included, would not want to trust any aspect
of their ministry with someone whom they do not
know. Spiritual covering helps to make you accountable. It gives you the opportunity and the means to
vet the musing of your quiet life with someone so
that your thought life is in order, and there is no danger that the devil can tempt you into isolation from

others.

The principle of spiritual covering is clearly illustrated in the Bible, though it is not known by that term. Much of the book of Exodus shows the relationship that Joshua had with Moses, who served as Joshua's spiritual covering. Elisha served as Elijah's apprentice and eventually succeeded him (I Kings 19:16-21). There is also the venerable relationship between Timothy and his mentor Paul in much of the book of Acts. And obviously, the relationship that Jesus had with his disciples is the most striking example of a spiritual covering in the scriptures.

A passage in 1 Peter 5 speaks of the character and responsibility of those who are disciples to others:

> *To the elders among you, I appeal as a fellow elder, a witness of Christ's sufferings and one who also will share in the glory to be revealed: Be shepherds of God's flock that is under your care, serving as overseers — not because you must, but because you are willing, as God wants you to be; not greedy for money, but eager to serve; not lording it over those entrusted to you, but being examples to the flock. And when the Chief Shepherd appears, you will receive the crown of glory that will never fade away.*

> *Young men, in the same way be submissive to those who are older. All of you, clothe yourselves with humility toward one another, because,*

"God opposes the proud but gives grace to the humble" (1 Peter 5:1-5).

These relationships are not simply for sharing of information or for teaching, but are an inherent part of the lifestyle of the kingdom. I have spiritual covering in my life, and I strongly recommend that you have it in yours. Some have condemned these spiritual-covering relationships because they have often been misused to abuse and gain unrighteous authority over others. But if they are managed according to 1 Peter 5:1-5, they bring spiritual blessings to both the shepherd and the flock, and should not be dismissed and rejected because of the sinful purposes of others.

Try not to fit in.

Okay, so given all the challenges that introverts face in an extroverted church, the temptation may exist to try to fit in by conforming to an extroverted lifestyle. After all, we may not be the life of the party, but we don't want to be left out of the party entirely. However, the one mistake that an introvert should not make is to try to fit in to an extroverted world. In many extroverted churches, there is pressure to go to every meeting, mingle with every person, speak at every opportunity, and minister to every person who walks in the church. In many of these churches, the more involved you are, the more spiritual you are, and the quiet, less hectic life of an introvert does not win Brownie points with many of these churches. For that reason, introverts often try to achieve some sense of belonging and demonstrate their spiritual growth by adhering to a hectic, fast-paced schedule, which only wears them out and leaves them little time for those quiet, reflective moments they cherish so much.

There are times when an introvert must become extroverted. As I mentioned previously, most introverts have some degree of extroversion in them and can function as such when necessary. But, as a rule, introverts should not try to deny their God-given temperament by trying to function wholly as extroverts in order to fit in at an extroverted church. This will only lead to confusion and frustration.

The story of Naomi in the book of Ruth has traditionally been examined for its kinsman-redeemer aspect. However, there is another important lesson in Naomi's life that is important to point out. Naomi was a woman from Bethlehem who moved to Moab with her husband and her two sons because of famine in Bethlehem. Moab was a heathen nation, likely chosen because of its proximity to Judah, and because of its fertility of land.

Naomi's husband Elimelech died, leaving her with her two sons. While in Moab, Naomi's two sons married Moabite women, one named Orpah, and the other named Ruth. After ten years, the two sons died also, leaving Naomi alone with her daughters-in-law.

At some point, Naomi decided to return to the land of Bethlehem, her native land, after the famine had lifted. On the way there, she turned to her daughters and urged them to return to their land. Orpah eventually decided to return, but Ruth persisted in staying with Naomi.

Some might question why Naomi decided to return to her land. After all, she was too advanced in age to have a husband. She knew that the likelihood of her daughters-in-law finding husbands that would take care of them was greater in Moab than it would be in Bethlehem. In Bethlehem, the daughters would be considered strangers and foreigners. They would be unlikely to find husbands who would want to marry heathen women. It would have been a lot easier for Naomi to stay in Moab where she could marry off her daughters and have the blessing of extended family, at least.

But Naomi knew who she was. She was a woman of God from the town of Bethlehem. She had no desire to compromise and live in a town of heathen people, just so life could be easier. She had no desire to fit in. Whatever it cost, she had to go back to the place where God wanted her to be. She had to be true to herself and to who God made her to be.

I once gave a sermon where I shared the differences between a two-prong and a three-prong electrical outlet. Many houses built before the 1950s still have the old two-prong outlets, but they are making many modern appliances with the new, standard three-prong plugs. To make the three-prong plugs work, many people pull out the grounding prong so that the plug will now fit in the two-prong outlet. So, in order to make the three-prong plugs work, people *materially alter* the plugs so that they fit into the old outlets. In order for the plugs to fit, the appearance and function of the plug was affected. The plug was once a grounding plug with three prongs. Now, with two prongs, it is no longer a grounding plug, and it is not serving its full purpose.

Human beings do the same thing at times. In order to fit in at places where we do not belong, we have to alter our function and purpose. So, introverts, in order to fit in, often try to be something they are not, and as such, alter the purpose and function for which God created them.

Naomi knew the value of being true to herself. She would not alter herself, becoming a Moabite and worshipping their gods, in order to fit in. Similarly, introverts, in order to be happiest, must not compromise on who they are and try to become extroverted in order to fit in to an extroverted world.

Prayer and meditation.

Prayer and meditation can be many things to many people. One widely accepted definition is that prayer is *communication and relationship with God.* Prayers can take on many forms and many types. As far as introverts are concerned, they sometimes have the same issues with talking to God as they do with talking with people.

I find that my prayer life is more robust and genuine when I do it alone. When I am asked to pray publicly, often there is the pressure of praying "like the hypocrites do." I feel as if I need to pray a long, loud, and emotional prayer in order for it to matter. For instance, if I'm asked to pray for someone's healing at a service, I may only have a few, simple words to say. But, a prayer that would normally take me only a minute to utter takes me five minutes when I utter it aloud, because of my need to impress others and seem more spiritual. A short prayer may seem less passionate and less meaningful, although that is not necessarily true.

When I am alone, I find that my prayers are short, stripped of all fat, and straight to the point. And I believe God hears them, because we do not need a bunch of words to get a prayer through. What really matters to God is not the length of your prayer, but how much it reflects your genuine faith in God.

Jesus said that the kingdom of God belongs to those who in their hearts and souls have the humility and innocence of little children. I have a five-year-old goddaughter who loves to pray. As I watch her pray, I can see how she genuinely desires to connect with God, even though her prayers rarely last longer than a minute. I look at her and find it hard to believe that God is ignoring her prayers just because they are not as lengthy and eloquent as many adult prayers.

Many introverts love to pray and meditate, and many excel at it because of their desire for solitude and internal reflection. But in order to function successfully, introverts need to pray in ways that are more compatible for them. Prayer meetings that consist of loud, long prayers and open sharing are not ideal for introverts, although they may be cathartic for extroverts.

This is an opportunity to convince the leadership of your church to start a prayer meeting designed for introverts, if one does not already exist. The meeting should not focus on conversation or other activities, but on praying silently and meditating on God.

Another option is to attend or organize regular retreats. Even the word *retreat* itself means a different thing to an extrovert than it does to an introvert. I have been on both types of retreats. Extroverted retreats tend to focus on activity and fellowship, while introverted retreats focus on communing with God and meditating in a quiet, unobtrusive atmosphere. The only thing that both types of retreats have in common is that both of them involve getting away from the hustle and bustle of everyday life and going to a peaceful place, usually out of town.

About fifteen years ago, I attended a retreat sponsored by the Church of the Nazarene. The retreat was held at the Dayspring Silent Retreat Center in Germantown, Maryland. I attended the retreat with about seven of my coworkers at a Nazarene mission called Community of Hope. The retreat center was a huge swath of land with beautiful fields, forests, streams, and ponds, with one rustic lodge used for dining and meeting. The retreat lasted for six hours, of which thirty minutes was for lunch, and another thirty was for reflection and praying together. The other five hours? Silent time to walk in the fields, sit beside the stream, or pray in the shade. If we passed by another individual during these times, *we could not say anything to them*. The focus was on silent and solitary meditation and reflection.

Several years later, I had an entirely different retreat experience. This one was held at the Sandy Cove Retreat Center in North East, Maryland. Sandy Cove is a beautiful family retreat center nestled along the Chesapeake Bay, and certainly has many areas where one could reflect silently on God. But this retreat, which lasted three days, was not focused on reflection, but on activity and community. Much of the three days was spent in praise and worship services and other meetings. There were three services per day, from 9:00 a.m. until 10:00 p.m., separated only by mealtimes and an hour or so here and there for personal time. There was little time for silent reflection, even though the accommodations in the main lodge had no Internet access and no TV. During break times, you were encouraged to fellowship and interact with others, especially those you did not know.

These two different types of retreats reflect the diverging values of introverts versus extroverts. As an introvert, I found that the Dayspring retreat was refreshing, whereas the Sandy Cove retreat left me drained. Both meetings had their benefits, and I was blessed by each. Yet it was clear that the Sandy Cove meeting was designed for extroverts, just as the Dayspring Silent Retreat Center would appeal more to introverts.

Introverts need both types of meetings, but introverts should seek out opportunities for silent worship and reflection, and should talk with church leadership about including more of these opportunities in retreats and in prayer meetings.

Another opportunity for introverts who want to be involved in ministry is to volunteer for the church prayer box team. A church prayer box is a locked box in which congregants can place their written prayer requests, which are usually anonymous. On a regular basis, a church leader opens the box and the prayer requests are distributed to one or more members of a prayer team, so they can pray for the requests in their daily prayers. The requests are kept confidential, and are destroyed once they have been prayed for. This is a great ministry for introverts, as it allows them to pray for the members of their congregation and for others, in their own way and in their own time, without personal contact.

Of course, if none of these options work, the introvert can always pray for his or her leaders and church during regular prayer time, knowing that God will answer faithful, righteous prayers.

Seek to understand extroverts.

> *There is neither Jew nor Greek, slave nor free, male nor female, for you are all one in Christ Jesus (Galatians 3:28).*

As much as I have portrayed in this book how extroverts often misunderstand introverts, the opposite is also true. Misunderstanding another person's temperament can lead to stereotyping and hindered fellowship. The tendency of some introverts to view extroverts as loud, intrusive, and insensitive will hinder the development of community and may cause introverts to form antagonistic cliques. However, when introverts seek to maintain community with extroverts, the body of Christ can be more effective in witness, in service, and in fellowship. Success in the body of Christ depends on introverts finding their place and understanding that extroverts have their place as well, and that both temperaments can flow together in harmony.

No Makeover for Christian Introverts

There is no one conclusive, definitive source of information as to the percentage of introverts in the world's population, but online research causes me to believe that the percentage is 25 percent. Some studies say that the number could be as high as 50 percent. In either event, it is clear that introverts occupy a significant chunk of the world's population. And while God can change introverts into extroverts, most introverts were wired this way by God, and can be a tremendous asset to his kingdom. Introversion is neither evil, nor weird, nor antisocial, nor shy, nor fear-based. It is a personality, placed in you by God, and an inherent part of your unique design. It is my hope and prayer that introverts who read this book will come away convinced that nothing is wrong with them and that God can use them just as they are. It is also my hope and prayer that extroverts who read this book will have a greater understanding of their quieter neighbors and not be driven by the need to change them into extroverts. God is building his kingdom with a cross-pollination of believers: young and old; rich and poor; men and women; foreign and domestic; black and white; introverted and extroverted. The beauty of God is that he can use everyone and draw each person into a community that will cause a fragrant aroma of worship. Though the methods will vary, both introverted and extroverted people can be used to do the work of ministry, including traditionally extroverted works such as evangelism, preaching, and pastoring. Everyone, no matter how he or she is wired by God, has a place in the kingdom of God.

Too many people these days, including Christians, are tempted to be something they're not. They want to make themselves into an image of something or someone else other than Christ. It is my hope and prayer that if you are an introvert, the words of this book have comforted your soul and convinced you that as long as you are operating within God's redemptive purpose, you have no need for a makeover to transform you into an extrovert. God created you as an introvert. You are fearfully and wonderfully made. Be proud of it and make the most of it.

I am.

Additional Resources

Below are a few additional resources on the subject of introversion. Inclusion of a resource on this list does not neccesarily imply endorsement by the author.

McHugh, Adam. *Introverts in the Church: Finding Our Way in an Extroverted Culture.* **IVP Books, 2009.**

Cain, Susan. *Quiet: The Power of Introverts in a World that Can't Stop Talking.* **Crown, 2012.**

Laney, Marti Olsen. *The Introvert Advantage: How to Thrive in an Extrovert World.* **Workman, 2002**

Helgoe, Ph.D, Laurie. *Introvert Power: Why your Inner Life is your Hidden Strength.* **Source Books, 2008**

Dembling, Sophia. *The Introverts Way: Living a Quiet Life in a Noisy World.* **Perigee Trade, 2012.**

Okerlund, Nancy. *Introverts at Ease: An Insider's Guide to a Great Life on your Terms.* **CreateSpace, 2011.**

Buelow, Beth L. *Insight: Reflections on the Gifts of being an Introvert.* **Introvert Entrepreneur, 2012.**

Ancowitz, Nancy. *Self-Promotion for Introverts: The Quiet Guide to Getting Ahead.* **McGraw-Hill, 2009.**

Bechtle, Mike. *Evangelism for the Rest of Us: Sharing Christ Within your Personality Style.* **Baker Books, 2006.**

Kahnweiler, Jennifer B. *The Introverted Leader: Building On Your Own Quiet Strength.* **Berrett-Koehler Publishers, 2009**

Laney, Psy.D, Marti. *The Introvert and Extrovert in Love: Making It Work When Opposites Attract.* **New Harbinger Publications, 2007.**

Baab, Lynne M. *Personality Type in Congregations.* **Alban Institute, 1998.**

Oswald, Roy M. *Personality Type and Religious Leadership.* **Alban Institute, 1988.**

www.ingramcontent.com/pod-product-compliance
Lightning Source LLC
Chambersburg PA
CBHW031339040426
42443CB00006B/389